A Modern Celt

Seeking the Ancestors

A Modern Celt

Seeking the Ancestors

Mabh Savage

Winchester, UK
Washington, USA

First published by Moon Books, 2013
Moon Books is an imprint of John Hunt Publishing Ltd., Laurel House, Station Approach,
Alresford, Hants, SO24 9JH, UK
office1@jhpbooks.net
www.johnhuntpublishing.com
www.moon-books.net

For distributor details and how to order please visit the 'Ordering' section on our website.

Text copyright: Mabh Savage 2012

ISBN: 978 1 78099 796 4

A CIP catalogue record for this book is available from the British Library.

Design: Lee Nash

Printed and bound by CPI Group (UK) Ltd, Croydon, CR0 4YY

We operate a distinctive and ethical publishing philosophy in all
areas of our business, from our global network of authors to
production and worldwide distribution.

CONTENTS

Acknowledgements

There are so many people who helped bring this book to fruition. Beatrix Faerber of CELT, thanks for your kind permission to use your fantastic website for sources; it truly has been invaluable. Chris, thank you for sharing your incredible insight and experience; this book draws upon it deeply and I am eternally and immensely grateful. Emma, you encourage me to keep writing and you shared something deeply personal with me and have allowed me to share it with others, thank you! Kath, thank you for proof-reading my initial excerpt and lending your insight and encouragement, your wisdom is inspiring and I thank you for letting me draw upon it when I have needed to. Fi, our long chats and the guidance you have given me have helped more than you can possibly know! Gez, you are my brother from another mother, enough said. Andy, you really are wiser than you know, and your words are true and moving, thanks for being my friend and listening to me waffle. Dan, your honesty and hopefulness are inspiring, thanks for picking up the phone whenever I needed you to. Kiera, our long email discussions are all filed away for me to go back to again and again, thanks for bearing with my ramblings! Cath, thank you for sharing your healing experiences, you describe it beautifully. And thanks for being one of my eleventh hour proof-readers along with Liz, Kay, Tara and Pippa – you guys rock! Mum, Dad, Conal, Kirsten; thank you for more than I can say here. Neil, you are my rock. Nathan, you are my sun, my son.

Introduction

I want to take you on a journey into the hearts and minds of people who, for whatever reason, feel a close connection to their Celtic ancestors and forebears. We're going to explore those reasons, and look at what drives this passion to connect with an ancient culture that has little or no resemblance to our lives today. Celtic tradition is at the heart of so many aspects of popular modern Pagan paths, and aspects of Celtic influence can be found daily in so much that we do.

This book aims to draw those aspects together and examine the relevance of such an ancient culture in modern day society. This is not a historical examination of the Celts; it's about how our ideas of Celtic society, mythology and beliefs influence us *right now*, and just as crucially about people's personal experiences with figures from Celtic mythology.

I'm lucky enough to have been raised by parents who were fascinated by Irish Celtic history and mythology, the two of which are often hard to separate. As a child I took for granted terms such as Tír na nÓg and Tuatha Dé Danann, then when I hit school I realised it was not common at all to be tied up in the ancient myths and legends of your great grandfathers. It wasn't until some years later that I managed to find (or was found by) people who shared my (and my family's) fascination for the Irish Celtic myths, and actively sought out ways to connect with their ancestors, and the gods and supernatural beings those ancestors would have revered or feared depending on the situation and their allegiances.

I started to learn the many facets of the Tuatha Dé Danann, and how these show themselves in our everyday lives. I began to realise that some of these stories are alive, not simply because we still tell them, but because in some ways we are still living them. I hope to share some of these realisations with you here, not in the desire that you feel the same, but with the hope that maybe you will be inspired to seek out a part of your own heritage, and discover if connecting to your past, your own personal history, can have a positive impact on your life.

Not all these epiphanies have been easy, and hard work and emotional exhaustion have gone hand in hand, down a tumultuous path that I cannot yet see the end of. Yet like anything arduous, one grows from it. In the physical world the uphill path stretches and improves the legs and constitution; so I feel my mental constitution is more robust, more ready to deal with the everyday and the extraordinary alike. This book will examine my experiences, and those of others who have discovered the Celtic roots within their own spiritual path. The ancestors themselves will speak to you (that's my Mum and Dad), and I hope to draw your attention to some everyday sights that show how ingrained some leftovers from Celtic culture have become. We'll start with how I got here, and quickly move to the present. With one foot in the past, come with me as we walk this bridge across millennia, to a time when all Celts are modern.

Chapter One

From Here to Eternity –
The Children of Danu

I never really referred to myself as a Pagan until I was in my early twenties. I always thought of myself as a witch, and I guess even with this I had my own definition. I know some people shy away from using the word *witch* because of its many negative connotations, but seeing as my path, or set of beliefs, wasn't really something I discussed with, well, anyone (not even some family members until quite recently), it didn't seem to matter. Meeting other likeminded, or similar minded people led me into the somewhat dubious habit of referring to myself as a Pagan, simply to help others pigeon hole me.

I'm not sure I actually fit the current definition of Pagan, seeing as most definitions you find will refer to the religious aspects of the term, and I do not think of myself as particularly religious. Understanding the changing of the seasons and the way the world transforms as it turns is not a religion. What I practise is about delight, celebration and respect; worship (which seems to be at the heart of most religions) has very little part to play in it.

In recent years I *have* been drawn more towards particular deities, and have to concede that this may be the first formation of some semblance of religious devotion. However, if life's path drew me away from this I would celebrate that life in the same way I do now. I don't so much 'believe' in gods and goddesses, but accept their existence; I've always found that belief implies doubt, and I have no doubts about the beings that share my world with me. It doesn't matter to me at all what others choose to put their faith in, or invite into their lives, except when I am sharing that experience with others directly. It's these shared experiences that have brought me closer to my Celtic heritage than I ever thought possible.

If you go to any Pagan gathering and ask ten different people what being a Pagan means to them, you will most likely get ten completely different answers! But I do practice witchcraft; I do follow the wheel of the year and celebrate the festivals accordingly and have done since I was a very young child, so because many Pagans do this I guess I fall into that bracket. So why, here, does it seem that I refer to myself as a Celt? A modern Celt?

Really that's an oxymoron, as the term Celt is a point of historical reference for a people that no longer exist; people who came to our shores from across Europe and possibly the Far East, bringing magic and mysticism which has been absorbed into history, tales and legends. When I speak about being a modern Celt, I'm referring to the aspects of the Celtic world that have survived into the 21st century; the festivals such as Samhain and Lughnasadh; art; beautiful poetry; magic, mystery and the stories and legends of their gods and spirits, including the race of beings known as the Tuatha Dé Danann.

... they landed with horror, with lofty deed,
in their cloud of mighty combat of spectres,
upon a mountain of Conmaicne of Connacht.

Without distinction to discerning Ireland,
Without ships, a ruthless course
the truth was not known beneath the sky of stars,
whether they were of heaven or of earth.[1]

This excerpt highlights a key point for me; this uncertainty as to whether the Tuatha Dé Danann are truly otherworldly, or simply so fierce and unstoppable that they seem more than human: like phantoms; like spirits from another world. The Book of Invasions (Lebor Gabála Érenn) is broadly accepted as a fictitious version of the history of Ireland and, of course, having been written over a millennia after Iron Age Celts settled in Ireland, in a time when most history and legend was passed through word of mouth, there is no way to really say how much is exaggeration, and how much is fantasy. Perhaps this is part of the attraction; the history is debateable; even the legends themselves have many versions that are all well documented today.

It's tantalising to imagine that there really could have been a race of people, of beings so wild and unearthly as to inspire immense fear into an entire culture (The Fir Bolg in this case). The thought that humans themselves could have inspired such stories and legends is for me, in some ways, more exciting than the thought of a supernatural race. Imagine that in 2000 years' time you are thought of as so superior, so extraordinary, that you must be a god: heady stuff.

I don't want to confuse you – am I telling you that they are gods (and goddesses) or not? Do I revere and worship them, or not? I guess the best way to explain how I understand the Tuatha Dé Danann and their relationship to our universe is to look at some of the key characters from Irish legend; we can explore a few facets of how they manifest themselves in a modern world, and what benefit this can have.

The Morrigan: Bloody Queen of Battle

Streaming red
Cloak of hair
Like yarn spun wild
For a coat of dreams
Of war and time
To pass the line
The blood along
Like velvet wine
Lady great and fierce of heart

Builds you up then tears apart
Protect thyself but know her if you can.
Devotional verse for the Morrigan, 2012

Let me introduce you to the Morrigan. Well, I can't really. You will either know her at some point in your life, or you won't, and really, that's entirely up to you and her. It's possible she may be a presence you haven't even recognised. Ever felt that red mist rise up behind your eyes with very little prompting? Ever felt a fierce passion in what would normally be a dispassionate context, like the sudden urge to kiss in the cold rain?

In my experience, people I know have been drawn to the Morrigan for many different reasons; these people who feel this strong connection to her seem to gravitate together, sometimes becoming connected in ways that have little or nothing to do with their spiritual path at all. She is the phantom queen, a great red haired warrior who is fierce in battle, wielding sword and spell with equal ferocity. She is the dark haired maiden, scrubbing shirts by the ford, a prophetess, and a doomsayer. She is fear and anxiety, but also the resignation of things to come. She is the raven on the battlefield, plucking the eyes from fallen heroes, reminding us we are all the same in the end, and also that war and violence can be necessary, but may be futile. A really great book to read to explore all these aspects is The Guises of the Morrigan by Sorita d'Este and David Rankine. My goal here, however, is to tell you what it's like to experience her; face to face, toe to toe, and still be in a fit state to write the experience down!

The Morrigan was one of the first mythical creatures I ever knew of that related directly to the Book of Invasions, although I didn't know it at the time. I was reading The Weirdstone of Brisingamen by Alan Garner and the evil witch in the story is named The Morrigan. Like most baddies in kids' books she's a fascinating character; even though the similarity to the figure in ancient mythology is slim, well done to Garner for getting children like me to sit up and take notice of the names that come from our history and our legends, as of course it prompted me to ask questions and discover who the real Morrigan is.

After years of distant appreciation, I was literally astounded when I discovered that the first Pagan group I ever worked with took the Morrigan as their tutelary goddess. Here I was, apparently by chance, in a group of people who had made her the focus for all things magical. I had spent a great many years at this point being cynical and doubtful of many ideas that I had previously taken for granted. I had become wary of the idea of a presence of any sort of energy one may refer to as fate, or destiny, or the idea of being on a path where one is supposed to be.

This single incident alone pushed me closer to the idea of external forces guiding us than probably any other event in the past ten years. It was as if someone had said, OK, you want to know about your Celtic roots? Well let's introduce you to one of them and see what happens!

I've made her sound terrible and formidable, as indeed she is, but there is more to her than that. She is also a mother figure, and in modern popular culture is sometimes portrayed as being 'with child' in her dealings with other beings or humans.[2] She is very sexual, and her sexual pursuits are often an integral part of legend. She is widely recognised as having a triple form, as many other 'popular' goddesses do – though I don't find her easy to simply put into the 'maid, mother, crone' goddess pot, although certainly at one time or another she clearly employs all these forms.

> Badb and Macha, greatness of wealth, Morrigu–
> springs of craftiness,
> sources of bitter fighting
> were the three daughters of Ernmas.[3]

Wealth, craft and violence are describing the three aspects of the daughters of Ernmas, often seen as three separate aspects of the one Morrigan. Often this is modified to Badb, Macha and Nemain, and Morrigan is used as a name for all the aspects put together.

I don't like to say one is right and another is wrong; I have found solace and understanding in many of her aspects, and believe that she is ever changing: mysterious and elusive. Even in Garner's book, she is portrayed as a shape shifter, and I think that is one of the keys to understanding her: she will change and you have to keep up with that change, or at least accept it, in order to understand it. If you reflect upon this, you will see that this is a very human idea; you are constantly changing and growing, therefore becoming a different person. As well as changing to develop ourselves in some way, we also change who we are depending on the situation we are in. We often use masks, figurative or otherwise (think about how you dress for work compared to a day around the house perhaps) and we change our manner to please others, or indeed to aggravate them.

We don't often admit to ourselves that we are doing this, and this is where the Morrigan may confront you; she forces you to face yourself, to see *you* as you really are, whether you like it or not! She can be cruel, but often it really is the old cliché of 'cruel to be kind'. There are some things you may have hidden about yourself, and she may shed light on them; other parts of yourself (such as insecurity or a tendency to try to please everyone) may fall into darkness as she takes you on the journey you need to go on.

One of my mentors once referred to her as the 'Domestos' of goddesses. This is a very apt metaphor for this book I think: in a modern world, she steps in and helps you spring clean; getting rid of the dust and clutter within one or many aspects of your life. These may be bad habits, destructive people, or the hundreds of other things we cling to in the false conviction that they are needed, that they are somehow 'part of our lives'. She gives you the power to say no, to walk away, but also to grasp hold of the things you need and the things you have to draw close to yourself.

She expects commitment and a true word, and you feel that she will be watching you as you watch yourself. If you say you are throwing something out then you better mean it, because she can be utterly devastating to those who go back on their word. *But isn't this just me being hard on myself for failing?* I hear the intelligent and cynical self-analyst say. Well, of course it is. All your power comes from within you at some level. The Tuatha Dé Danann aren't there to mollycoddle you or pick you up and set you on your path. They're there to remind you that *you* are the power in your life, and to fail in a promise to one of them is to fail yourself miserably.

The Morrigan is in some ways easily related to as the personification of our 'fiery' emotions; anger, lust, passion, the need for justice, protectiveness, love, creativity and excitement. She is also linked to deception and vindictiveness, and if you read some of the tales about her you will understand this.

Then came the Morrígu, daughter of Ernmas, from the elf-mounds in the guise of an old woman and in Cú Chulainn's presence she milked a cow with three teats. The reason she came thus was to be succoured by Cú Chulainn, for no one whom Cú Chulainn had wounded ever recovered until he himself had aided in his cure. Maddened by thirst, Cú Chulainn asked her for milk. She gave him the milk of one teat. 'May this be swiftly wholeness for me'. The one eye of the queen which had been wounded was cured. Cú Chulainn asked her for the milk of another teat. She gave it to him. 'Swiftly may she be cured who gave it'. He asked for the third drink and she gave him the milk of the third teat. 'The blessing of gods and non-gods be on you, woman'. — The magicians were their gods and the husbandmen were their non-gods. — And the queen was made whole.[4]

Prior to this excerpt, the Morrigan came to the hero Cú Chulainn in the guise of a heifer, an eel and finally a wolf seeking to destroy him, but he wounded her gravely each time. In the section on the previous page she uses further transformation and the strength of his greatest desire at this time – his overwhelming thirst – to trick him into healing her. Despite the fact that he knows from the battle previously that the Morrigan clearly has the power of shape shifting, he is not suspicious. Or, if he is suspicious, he is so desperate for succour that he is uncaring of the situation.

I suppose it's possible that in his tired and parched state, that it doesn't occur to him that the great Morrigan would ever consider portraying herself as old and feeble. He is grateful and sincerely wishes the old woman well, and his sincerity heals the wounds he originally caused. The messages within this story are numerous, but what I take from it is that a lack of pride at times can be a powerful shield; posing as a powerful creature only brought the Morrigan pain and suffering, but posing as the old woman brought her charity and kindness.

Sometimes we should give into the more fragile aspects of our character, and not be afraid to let them show, and we may find some of the things we need coming to us. I know people who are afraid to show certain kinds of affection, because they think it makes them look weak, or foolish. And even though they feel strong, and independent, they are lonely; they freely admit this, and feel they are better off in the long run. If that is true, well I say good luck to them. But perhaps letting down their guard, and letting someone get close, could be a wonderful thing? A new experience to be treasured?

I think often it is fear that stops us changing ourselves and transforming ourselves; not into another external shape, like the wolf or the eel, but into a different creature inside. We become scared of rejection, scared of change, scared of being too hard and above all too many of us fear the opinion of others. The Morrigan shows here the benefit of letting yourself change into something you never thought possible, never imagined you could be; and lo, she is healed.

The Dagda: Good God of the Club and Cauldron

There was a famous king of Ireland of the race of the Tuatha Dé, Eochaid Ollathair his name. He was also named the Dagda i.e. good god, for it was he that used to work wonders for them and control the weather and the crops. Wherefore men said he was called the Dagda.[5]

Here again is a figure with multiple faces, although the most obvious is of the fierce warrior, with his enormous club that could kill nine men in one blow. The other side of this coin is, apparently, he could also revive the mortally wounded with the handle of this club. Straight away we are talking about the inter-connectivity of life and death, and how in this world, one cannot exist without the other. The Dagda is, from this evidence, a metaphor for life itself; things die and things are born again, and without one the other would cease to be.

The Dagda was (is) also a musician, and closely connected with the turn of the seasons, and the onset of battle. Whoa, whoa, whoa I hear you cry! Where does it end? How can one deity encompass all this? And how can you draw upon something that has such ever-changing facets? It's like reaching into the cupboard to get the coffee only to find it has changed to tea, then the next day to sugar!

Well, this is why I have already mentioned the possibility that the Tuatha Dé Danann are a *people*, a race of earthly beings, rather than deities in the truest sense. Here's an exercise to help you understand what I mean: think of anyone you know, that you are reasonably close to. Tell me three things about them. Now take each of those three points e.g. they are kind; they can have a bad temper; they like to play football. Now tell me three details about each of those points.

We'll take kindness as our first example. You know they like dogs, because they have one which they love to pieces. You know they give to a charity for homeless people. And when you were short of cash, they lent you some money, although they were keen to get it back as soon as you could afford it. So that's three aspects of kindness right there. With regards to their bad temper, you heard them shouting at their brother once, in a fierce argument about a wager. You heard that they took gleeful revenge upon someone who played a practical joke on them at work. They also didn't talk to you for a week when you couldn't give them back the money you owed them! So there we go: even though we have only covered kindness and temper, we have already uncovered so many facets of this person's personality.

Now think about a deity or spiritual being, regardless of whether or not they are a part of a mythological cycle; *why should they be any different?* Every deity has multiple facets. The Tuatha Dé Danann are characterised by the fact that these facets are curiously human; the Dagda's love of music coupled with the turning points of battles; these are very specific and focused points that paint a picture of a powerful yet worldly being; the Dagda is not above the concerns of humans as some deities appear to be, because these are *his* concerns, his battles, and indeed, his songs.

So again, how do we draw on this? Well, if you were in a situation where you wanted to calm yourself about your own fear of mortality, perhaps you could think of the Dagda and his club which causes both life and death, and use that as a focus point for a meditation on how death is an intrinsic part of life, and death is just another turning point in the cycle you cannot help but be caught in. Hmm, that's a bit deep perhaps for an 'everyday' example; maybe you are just having a hard time dealing with a mistake that you have made; perhaps you dealt with someone rashly at work, and are reaching within yourself to find the strength to see the correct course of action.

'Put the staff in my hand,' said the Dagda. And they lent him the staff, and he put the staff upon them thrice, and they fell by him, and he pressed the smooth end upon his son, and he arose in strength and health. Cermait put his hand on his face, and rose up and looked at the three dead men that were before him.

'Who are these three dead men before thee?' said Cermait.

'Three that I met,' said the Dagda, 'sharing their father's treasures. They lent me the staff, and I slew them with one end, and I brought thee to life with the other end.'

'That is a sad deed,' said Cermait, 'that they should not be brought to life by that which caused me to live.'

The Dagda put the staff upon them, and the three brothers arose in health and strength.[6]

This excerpt from 'How the Dagda got his Magic Staff' shows a rash and desperate action, but rooted in that most noble firmament – love. Yet the object of his love, his son, is honest and hard enough to tell this great warrior he has done wrong, so the Dagda corrects his mistake, even knowing the retribution for his original actions may be great.

Stories such as these reach out to us, even today, as they speak of flawed, human reactions to extraordinary situations. They help us understand our own reactions, and sometimes make us glad of the way we already are, by holding our own standards up against some less than desirable behaviours! Likewise, if we found ourselves behaving in this rash manner, we would hope that this type of story would move us to improve the situation either by action or words. I think all of us have been Cermait at some point: forced to tell a loved one that they have done wrong.

The Dagda, like the Morrigan, also has a prominent sexuality, and by that I mean his lust is sometime very prominent, as is his, er, equipment! Many images show the huge stature of his club being mirrored by the equally huge stature of his penis. Perhaps the idea that one end of his club can give life is a little more complex (or simple – depending on your viewpoint) than just touching the wood to a dead body; perhaps there is the implication that the Dagda gives life by the simplest and most well-known way; through sex! Something most adults can relate to.

Sex is a way of becoming close to someone, or indeed the result of the same, and also of course it should be fun, exciting, exhilarating. A deity that is seen to be powerful sexually not only is showing that he gives life but that he is full of life, he embraces life, he is capable of spontaneity and representative of giving into wilder urges and desires. Sometimes, it is good for us to be in touch with the parts of ourselves we restrain at times; the need to twirl and dance and laugh; the desperate urge to sing at the top of our lungs, or the yearn to scream and beat our fists against something when we feel frustrated or angry. Most of us strive for some sort of balance, and balance means accepting these parts of one's self and giving them a place in your life.

The fact that the Dagda has a club and a cauldron straight away paints a picture of a god that carries symbols for both male and female fertility. As king of the Tuatha Dé Danann and the ruler of Ireland maybe this is how he ensures the fertility of the land and keeps it eternally renewed. I think we can draw upon this strength to renew ourselves, not necessarily sexually, but to literally breathe new life into things that have maybe gone stale for us: relationships; projects; a place that has lost something for us. We can use the imagery and the energy the Dagda creates to detect the beauty and the power in these situations, and move ourselves forward with a heightened sense of contentment.

Brigid: Songs, Sons and Smithies

Brigit, that was a woman of poetry, and poets worshipped her, for her sway was very great and very noble. And she was a woman of healing along with that, and a woman of smith's work, and it was she first made the whistle for calling one to another through the

night. And the one side of her face was ugly, but the other side was
very comely. And the meaning of her name was Breo-saighit, a fiery
arrow.[7]

Interestingly my first direct working within the group I fell in
with was not actually focusing on Morrigan, but on the goddess
Brigid. The name of many pronunciations! Even in a ritual
setting I have heard her name perhaps pronounced three
different ways, but indeed it does seem that she has had many
incarnations over the years so perhaps this is appropriate. St
Brigid of Kildare, one of Ireland's patron saints, is a possible
Christianisation of this triple goddess of spring, and indeed they
share the same feast day at the start of February. St Brigid was
the patron saint of farmers, smiths and children: yet more links
to her faerie forebear.[8]

It's not a huge jump to see links to Persephone in Brigid's
legend too, furthering the theories that the Celts who settled in
Ireland had indeed travelled greatly across Europe and the
Mediterranean, absorbing aspects of the religion and culture in
and around areas such as Greece. Both Persephone and Brigid
are daughters of 'kings of gods' – Persephone is Zeus's daughter,
while Brigid is daughter of the Dagda, and both are strongly
associated with the springtime.

Brigid is an Irish goddess who tells a very human story. She
works with smiths, bards, healers and farmers and others who
create something not simply for themselves.[9] Festivals for her
bring communities together in anticipation of the coming spring
and defeat of winter; in celebration of the fertility of the land and
indeed of the young women who dance in her honour. Dolls are
made and fires are burned all to show that though the cold
months are not quite through, the human spirit is not only
surviving but thriving.

Her story tells that as the daughter of the Dagda, she was
born at daybreak, rising into the sky with fire burning in her

hand, spreading sunlight across the land. Later in her tale she marries Bres of the Fomorians, hoping to achieve unity and a peace between the two peoples. Her sons are great warriors, and when one dies on the battlefield it is Brigid's grief-stricken keening that prevents further bloodshed.[10]

She is the power and passion of a parent; the enormous love that you can have for one person or one group of people, and the ability to show that love and emotion unashamedly. She is hard work; grafting for something you need, something you want, or simply for pleasure. She is the delight in the simplest meal shared with a loved one, and the joy in the most elaborate feast. She is the soul of song, and the muse to all musicians. She is fire being built in the morning, the kindling of new thoughts and ideas; the ember still glowing in the hearth at the end of a hard day; the spark of desire; the beginning of things, and the reflection on what has gone before. She is honesty and clarity, and the under-standing of necessary sacrifice.

Again, we are talking about an enormous amount of different aspects to one being, and in any situation where you bring one being or deity into focus e.g. for worship or meditation, it's worth considering these aspects, to make sure you are choosing the right person for the job. To generalise, Brigid is about produc-tivity and being the best you can be, which hopefully we can apply to many situations in all parts of our lives. As a musician, I have often found that after a ritual where Brigid has been present, I yearn to pick up the guitar or pen some lyrics, and have even found that after a previously 'dry' spell, where I found it hard to pluck songs and melody from the ether, my efforts suddenly become productive and fruitful.

I find Brigid's presence less forceful than, for example, the Morrigan's; she is less intimidating, but at the same time, somehow commanding just as much respect. Rather than being forced to self-analyse and strip away the layers to get to your core, Brigid encourages you to act, to do and to build; to keep your hands busy in the hope that your mind may follow. She brings clarity through creativity, reminding us that our skills and crafts are as much a part of our heritage and link to our ancestors as the written histories and stories we look to for clues to our beginnings.

Lugh: Long Arm, Fierce Shout

'I am Lugh, son of Cían of the Tuatha Dé Danann, and of Ethlinn, daughter of Balor, King of the Fomor,' he said; 'and I am foster-son of Tailltiu, daughter of the King of the Great Plain, and of Echaid the Rough, son of Duach.'

'What are you skilled in?' asked the door-keeper; 'for no one without an art comes into Teamhair.'

'Question me,' said Lugh; 'I am a carpenter.'

'We do not want you; we have a carpenter ourselves, Luchtar, son of Luachaid.'

'Then I am a smith.'

'We have a smith ourselves, Colum Cuaillemech of the Three New Ways.'

'Then I am a champion.'

'That is no use to us; we have a champion before, Ogma, brother to the king.'

'Question me again,' he said; 'I am a harper.'

'That is no use to us; we have a harper ourselves, Abhean, son of Bicelmos, that the Men of the Three Gods brought from the hills.'

'I am a poet,' he said then, 'and a teller of tales.'

'That is no use to us; we have a teller of tales ourselves, Ere, son of Ethaman.'

'And I am a magician.'

'That is no use to us; we have plenty of magicians and people of power.'

'I am a physician,' he said.

'That is no use; we have Diancecht for our physician.'

'Let me be a cup-bearer,' he said.

'We do not want you; we have nine cup-bearers ourselves.'

'I am a good worker in brass.'

'We have a worker in brass ourselves, that is Credne Cerd.'

Then Lugh said: 'Go and ask the king if he has any one man that can do all these things, and if he has, I will not ask to come into Teamhair.'[11]

This excerpt from Lady Gregory's retelling of the tales of the Tuatha Dé Danann says a great deal about the diverse nature of this deity, Lugh, known as the long armed because of his skill with the sling and spear, although there is reference to throwing the sacred Gae Bolga from the fork of the toes, rather than by hand.[12]

Lugh is a foster child, given by his father Cían to Tailltiu, who is actually one of the original Fir Bolg; the tribes inhabiting Ireland at the time the Tuatha Dé Danann begin their conquest of the land. According to the book of invasions, after Tailltiu dies Lugh commemorates her by performing games and singing a song of lamentation in her honour, showing his dedication to her. The festival, which lasts four weeks, is called Lughnasadh, and we'll cover this festival in more detail later on. Lugh goes on to rule Ireland, and destroys his own grandfather, Balor, with a stone thrown from a sling; a popular theme in folklore and mythology: the mighty king slain by a single blow from a simple weapon. As well as showing how the mighty can fall from a single, well placed blow, this highlighted Lugh's skill with the weapon, because Lugh had to ensure he hit Balor in his eye.

Lugh is strongly associated with hounds, and his own son is known as Cú Chulainn, which means 'Cullan's Hound'. Lugh is a strong leader; at the time he joins the Tuatha Dé Danann he is surprised that they have allowed themselves to become cowed by the invading Fomorians, and because of his fierceness in the face of repression he is given command and leads the Tuatha Dé

Danann to victory. He is not above deceit, as can be seen from the tale of the sons of Tuireann. The sons of Tuireann kill Lugh's father, Cían, for nothing other than bad blood between the families.

Cían has a heavy 'blood price' (a fine you pay to the victim's family when you have killed someone) although this is almost lost, as Cían is in the form of a pig when the sons of Tuireann, two of them also magically transformed into the form of hounds, find him. He begs to die in his own form or be spared. The eldest son, Brian, refuses to spare him (is in fact quite venomous about wanting him dead!) but allows him to revert to his own form. Cían has one bittersweet moment of triumph by telling them they will have to pay an extortionate blood price, as he has the highest blood price of anyone, anywhere, in any time.

Lugh knows who has killed his father, and he is heartbroken but resolute that Cían will be avenged. He advises the Tuireann brothers that all they need to get are some paltry items: pig skin, apples, that sort of thing. They agree, and then he reveals that every item on his seemingly innocuous list is actually a unique or magical item (in one case a unique person!) and the journey to get these items is so perilous they will certainly die. So it's win/win for Lugh. If they die, he has vengeance (or justice, depending on your outlook). If they get his items, he will be uniquely advantaged as he will own some of the most precious and useful items in the world, just as he is about to go into full-on battle with the Fomorians. This seems not only pretty underhand, but very cool and tactical thinking under enormous emotional stress.

It's nice to think that we're above revenge, and that justice should be fair and compassionate, but there are times in everyone's life I would think, when an eye for an eye seems the best way, even if it is only a passing thought that we squash with our better nature. I'm certainly not saying we should all rush out, vigilante style, to avenge the death of our loved ones, but it's good to recognise the vengeful side of ourselves. If it is inappropriate then we are only able to quash it if we accept it is there. Lugh follows his vengeful streak, and actually uses the whole situation to his advantage. I won't spoil the ending in case you want to go and have a look at The Sons of Tuireann; it's a great legend and well worth a read.

Lugh is also often seen as a sun god, perhaps because of his shining visage (literally, in one story it is asked, 'Is the sun rising in the west today?' and the reply is, 'No, that is the shining of the face of Lugh'[13]) and because of his strong association with the first harvest, Lughnasadh; pretty much the height of summer in this part of the world. I know that some who honour a god and goddess as a dual deity partnership, for example in some Wiccan paths, choose Lugh as their named God, the aspect of the male, as he can be seen as alive and rampant as the corn and harvest during the summer days, and also in the darker months as the hunter; mischief personified.

Lugh is loyalty, family and a keen sense of self-worth. He is skill, craft, cleverness and quickness with words. He is motivation to greatness and the courage to take chances: it takes guts to walk up to the doors of a great hall, in the lands of a great lord, and say, 'Got anyone better than me? I don't think so. Gimme the job!' But that's what he did, and he ended up a leader of his people; loved and revered, and feared by his enemies. Lugh is definitely a force you want in your life if you need a boost of courage, or just a nudge to remind you that what you're good at, you're *really* good at, and no one can take that away from you.

Cú Chulainn: A Very Human Demi God

And when the stars go out
You can hear me shout
'Two heads are better than none,
One hundred heads are so much better than one'.

I'm a boy who was born blind to pain
And, like a hawk, I'll swoop and swoop again.
I am the flash of Hawkeye in the sun.
When you see me coming you had
Better run . . . run . . . run . .
From Dearg Doom (Red Destroyer) by Irish band Horslips[14]

Cú Chulainn is an extremely interesting character from the Ulster Cycle with many links to the Tuatha Dé Danann. His tales weave a rich and vibrant thread in the tapestry of Irish history and mythology. His origin story is told in many different forms, but it's generally accepted that he is the son of Lugh, a god of the Tuatha Dé Danann and a great leader, and the charioteer Deichtine (daughter of Conchobar King of Ulster), a fierce and proud woman who possibly had the power to transform into a bird, along with her 50 maidens, according to varying forms of the tale.

Cú Chulainn seems on the surface violent, reckless and hungry for glory, and his tales are of battles and quests and difficulties overcome. Yet he is also fiercely loyal, a great friend and in need of love and approval. I'm lucky enough to have a great friend who is named for Cú Chulainn – indeed his family name 'McCullough' translates as 'The Son of the Hound of Ulster'.

I ask my friend, Chris, about his own origins and how it felt to discover the story behind his name sake.

He says: 'As I was growing up, I was Irish protestant. Always went to church, Sunday school; but through that my Dad always instilled in me: you've got a good name; you've got a proud name. It was only when I was a teenager he told me, 'You know what it means? It means Son of the Hound of Ulster.' It was only much, much later, into my thirties, that I looked into it: what *is* the Son of the Hound of Ulster? I didn't know. I found out that Cú Chulainn was the Hound of Ulster, so I am a descendant of his. So you look back, and you think, 'Yeah, I am the son of the hound of Ulster', and then you found out what Cú Chulainn done; his fights and his battles and his conquests; wow, that's some ancestor to have. And then to be given the mantle and given the prize of a demi-god, as the Greeks say; even though he was a mortal man he was the son of Lugh; sort of like Hercules. And to think that was my ancestor! Which he has to be because I'm carrying the name. I wouldn't have got it for nothing.'

I express how amazed I would have been to find something like that out; I know I have some faintly royal blood in my ancestry and am proud to know some of the story behind that, but to find out you are a living legacy of the Ulster Cycle... Wow, that's something else entirely. How did Chris feel about this?

Chris says: 'When I first found it out it was just something to be proud of: this is my name and this is what it means. Then I started following this [Celtic] path and looking into it a bit further and it meant a lot more. Especially when, through sheer coincidence, I happened upon a group that, well, I wouldn't say worshipped, but looked up to the Morrigan; and even then, I didn't make the connection.'

I want to break off here to comment on Chris's discomfort with the term worship; I think many people on a less monotheistic path have trouble with the term 'worship'. Worship implies utter devotion and sacrifice to the being or deity, whereas in my experience it has been more of a case of *honouring* the spirits, ancestors and deities.

Yes, as Chris says, looking up to them, as something greater than we are, but not necessarily *better* than us. We don't use them as role models; we want to be ourselves, but greater. We want to develop who *we* are, not become something else entirely. We look for guidance, not for answers. We are responsible for our own actions; we don't wait for a god, or being, or spirit to tell us what to do and what is right.

However, we listen and we learn. We follow the examples in the stories of our ancestors and when faced with similar trials, try not to make the same mistakes. We give offerings and thanks for bounty placed our way and make magic in the name of gods and spirits to move obstacles out of our way.

Is this worship? It seems more to me like younger siblings looking up to a big brother, or sister, and trying to reach for that greatness while also laughing at the antics when the big sibling gets it wrong. We see these beings reaching for greatness in the tales we tell and hand down through the years, and we promise ourselves we will reach just as high and far, but in our own endeavours, remaining true to our own desires. We stand on our own two feet but we're not ashamed to ask for help when we need it. We embrace our humanity, feel awe at that which is beyond us, but truly realise we have our own special place in the universe, just as the Tuatha Dé Danann do, and nothing, not even their majesty, can detract from that.

I wonder if Chris had any experience of the Morrigan before he found the group. Had his namesake Cú Chulainn led him to discover stories of the Morrigan already?

'No,' he says. 'I looked into the name of McCullough and that was it. That was as far as it got. What is McCullough? Son of the Hound of Ulster. OK, and the Hound of Ulster is Cú Chulainn. OK. What did he do in his life? Why is he so special?

'So I read the stories, and it was, 'Oh he goes in to battle, so on and so forth, the Morrigan comes down, etc. etc. and she changes her guises, and she's the washer at the ford,' and I'm thinking OK, it's just a story. This Morrigan character plays a good part in this story. The cattle raid; she played a part in that; here's that character again. And that's all she was; she was just another character *in* the story of Cú Chulainn.

'One night, after being invited to someone's house, they started passing around the horn, and you had to salute: give a salute to your ancestors. I'd never done anything like this before in my life. I thought, I'm reading about Cú Chulainn, so I'll do that. The horn came to me and I said, 'To my ancestor, Cú

Chulainn', and there were three people in that room whose faces dropped! Their jaws hit the floor. F**k. Who have we got in our presence? I didn't *know* who the Morrigan was. For those three people to stand and look at me going F**k. That's Cú Chulainn in the presence of the Morrigan, 'What have we got here?' And from that day onwards, I'm destined to follow this path to find out, how's it going to pan out? There has to be an answer, doesn't there.'

I wonder out loud if this is an incredible privilege and opportunity, or a terrifying responsibility.

'I'm very lucky. *Extremely* lucky. How many other McCulloughs are out there that either a) know the name and know what it means and live with it or b) haven't got a clue what it means? For that to fall to me, ah, brilliant.'

I know from my own experiences that the Morrigan can be a temperamental force, powerful and fierce in passion and emotion. With Chris honouring his ancestor, Cú Chulainn, does he ever find them pulling him in different directions? Is there a sense of conflict between these two powerful presences who have so much ancient history between them?

'At times there is a bit of conflict in decision-making, or in the outcome, but I think I've trained myself well to go with my gut. Roll with the punches, because I think that's what my ancestor would have done.'

I ask Chris if he felt there was some ancestral nudging, some coughs and whispers from the wings, to get him to where he is now; some supernatural prompting that led him to the people he now knows. Because I myself can't believe that I fell in with the same group of people, knowing my heritage (some of my heritage, anyway) and also how fascinated I had been with the Celtic tales since being a tiny child. I add that it doesn't feel like coincidence; it almost felt like something had been pushing me.

Chris thinks about this and responds: 'To fall in with that group, which so tied in with Cú Chulainn's life; well I thought, this is just history repeating itself. This is the other side playing out their lives through us mere mortals, like chess pieces. There has to be tugs; the veil between this and the next world is so thin; there has to be tugs somewhere. Tugs and pushes. If you were to sit down and really, really think back along your own life, the amount of decisions you've made, whether they be right or wrong, at that time they were the decisions to be made. Did you *make* that decision or were you slightly pushed in that direction? Were you nudged in a dream state and thought, 'Oh, I know what I'll do today! I'll do this'.

'Just because they're our ancestors: people think ancestors and they think of the dead; they think of hundreds and hundreds of years ago; but they're not. They're there; they're right beside you. Even your grandparents, they're your ancestors, and we are the ancestors of the future. So we in ourselves are ancestors, so the word ancestors can be taken out of context completely.'

I ponder that it's easy to forget that no matter what time you lived (or live) in, or how the trappings of day-to-day life may change, people are still people. They have the same sort of fears and dreams and hopes and that's why you *can* understand your ancestors and therefore your ancestors can understand you. If you're getting prods and pushes it's probably because they've been in a similar situation at some point in their own lives, although the settings and backdrops may have differed.

Chris replies: 'It's either that or they've got to that same point you are at now in their own lives and they made the *wrong* decision. In that case, they're saying, 'I know where you're going; you don't want to do that, you want to do this'. For several reasons; like you say, they've been there, they flipped the coin; they took the tail side; they never experienced the head side so they want to know what would have happened if they'd chosen differently. In the future you now know if you choose tails you do this; if you choose heads, you do *this*.

'But, as we know, every path has many forks. So on the tails side, on the red tablet, you've gone off and done this, which in itself caused this effect and that effect. On the heads side, OK, let's see what happens, I'm now down this path; oh, I've got another choice. Two separate, different choices from the ones I would have had down the other path. It's infinite – it blows your mind. So at each juncture, each choice, it just doubles, and doubles. So if you take that through the generations you've got plenty of time to work out what's right and what's wrong.'

This makes me wonder if we will also end up in this position, as sometime watchers and guardians of our descendants, seeing how our own lives potentially could have played out, through the actions of those who come after us. I ask Chris if he thinks we will get that opportunity.

'Yes,' he replies, 'if we haven't already done so. I know; it's a real mind f**k! Time has no significance!'

So, in essence, we could be getting the insight, the inspiration, either from our ancestors, because they knew what happened in their lives in a similar circumstance and want to help, or equally from our descendants, who have learnt from our own example!

Chris concludes: 'Yeah, it's a full circle isn't it? Where one life ends, another begins.'

So living with your ancestors may not just mean living, as Chris does, with the knowledge that he is descended from a great hero such as Cú Chulainn, and may not even just mean simply learning all you can about them, and trying to honour them by following their ways and traditions. We may actually be talking here about walking side by side with people who, to us and the way we perceive reality, died thousands of years ago, and who are simply a step away through a veil rarely breached within our lifetimes. Whether they *are* there or not, we certainly keep them alive with the fantastic tales and myths that abound about this fascinating culture.

So what's the relevance of all these stories in this modern age? How can we *possibly* relate to a world of human gods and goddesses, tribal disputes and deep, dark magic?

Well I guess there's a touch of sarcasm in my carefully chosen italic there, as the sentence kind of answers itself. We all aspire to be something greater than we are: every one of us. The idea of gods and goddesses not as distant, unreachable *enigmata*, but as real, emotional, flesh and blood and above all flawed beings is very attractive. We don't need standards to live up to which are handed to us with barely any explanation, but something which allows us to examine and judge ourselves.

The world is constantly torn by war and especially civil unrest, as seen so often on the news lately, so the stories of the warring Celtic tribes and the Book of Invasions (the 'history' of the many tribes that invade Ireland) seem to have a particular poignancy right now. And how can we not be enticed by the magic and mysticism; fantastic worlds of things just beyond the mind's eye? The lure of the Tuatha Dé Danann is in the combination of fantasy and reality; astonishing magical creatures caught in very human situations; war, love, sex and death. The best TV shows aspire to bring you all this in popcorn crunching glory but it's already here, combined with real-life lessons and a good dose of magic to boot. Each story can be a metaphor for something in your life, each being a personification of an attribute or skill you either want or need to bring into focus in your life.

Chapter Two

Turning the Wheel –
The Seasons and Celebrating Them

Thirty circles
Bold and bright
Ancient days and
Timeless night
Wasted moments
Treasured slice
Of life eternal
Entered thrice
As child, as maid
As mother fair.
As soul so heavy
Limp with care.
Dragging onward,
Cutting ruts
And dusty trails
In gore and guts;
The viscera of life's true trials
The lies and laughs
The way and wiles
Of those who tempt
And those you trust
Of what you need
And what you lust.
Now that rut it cuts both ways
A path you built through shining days
A light beside, a glow before: Lead on and find your core.

Right now I can walk to the end of the ginnel at the back of my house and stand by a deep hawthorn hedge, inhaling spring rain while my ears fill with the waterfall of birdsong from the robins and blackbirds that rustle gently through the green. Brambles creeping 'round me while cats watch from dripping wooden fences, stony skies close and wet, heavy with the promise of a storm. Cool air raising each hair on my arms, flattening my coat against my chest while my shoes sink slightly in the sodden soil, rooting me in place. Suspended in a web of being, a tiny speck of life in an endless universe; this is magical, wondrous; not grasping at understanding but accepting existence as a fact and a gift.

This feeling of being a part of the world, not just something walking upon it, is what lets us *feel* the changes as winter gives way to spring, and spring bursts into summer. The Celtic year is all about taking notice of the seasons; understandable when you realise that this originates from a time when not paying attention to the turning weather could mean planting food at the wrong times, a ruined harvest or even travelling into certain death. Starting an expedition just as winter is about to turn harsh could be lethal.

Now many people from many paths, not just those that actively embrace Celtic tradition, use this wheel of the year as a way to signpost and celebrate the key turning points of the year. The Celtic 'quarter year' festivals are the points, the 'sabbats' as many refer to them, that don't truly tie into any astronomical points of interest (because they tend to fall on the same dates each year although in the original Celtic calendar this would *not* have been the case), but roughly lay the year and the seasons into four sections, and also into dark and light; summer and winter, and try to mark the turning points in each.

Lambs in the Belly

Brigid, who is also known as Persephone
Rises like an epiphany
From the womb of Winter's death.[15]

One of the aforementioned turning points is Imbolc, celebrated at the start of February; roughly half way between winter solstice and spring equinox (in the northern hemisphere anyway – in the southern hemisphere this would be around the start of August, around the time we are celebrating Lughnasadh). This is the time of year when you really start to notice that, yes, the days *are* getting longer and lighter, and the air is beginning to warm.

Imbolc is a celebration of the coming spring, making it through the harshest part of winter, and a time to honour Brigid, a goddess who, like the Morrigan, is often revered in triple form, and has many aspects. As mentioned previously, she is a patron to bards, and indeed I have found my own music more forthcoming after working with her at Imbolc, and have even written a song solely dedicated to her and the coming spring. She is a goddess of fertility and birth; hardly surprising as she is associated so closely with the return of spring, and the lambing season's start.

She is the goddess of smithing and other crafts, and strongly linked with fire; it is no wonder at this cold, forbidding time of the year, when there is barely a warm breath to whisper of the spring to come, that such a person, such a goddess would be drawn close to people's hearts. To cook, to craft, to make love and to keep fires burning – such human things are what bring hope and help us survive when the elements are against us.

Today, many of us in the western world take warmth and shelter for granted, and have little to worry about in the way of food shortages. So what makes people like me turn to Brigid at Imbolc? The simple answer is this: the hunger and cold become a metaphor. Of course we don't want to be hungry, and we always make the wish that we never *literally* hunger, and that we may honour the earth so that she may not hunger – through protection of resources and responsibility.

However, we also look to our spiritual selves to make sure that side of us is not being starved, and by this I don't mean simply on a theological or 'otherworldly' plane, but simply how we behave in day-to-day life. Are we working so hard we run ourselves into the ground? Are we forgetting to take time out for our families? Have we lost touch with the things that make us who we are? Or are we happy, content in our life, working towards goals that are true, fit to ourselves and our purpose? Do we even know what that purpose is? Most people don't I guess; I'm pretty sure I change my mind every year!

This is a chance to celebrate if we have achieved over the winter what we set out to; that may be as simple as weathering the winter with family, safe and warm, or perhaps a project or goal that we have been working towards. Sometimes it will be to remember oaths or goals that were set in place at previous festivals, often the previous Imbolc. Brigid is a point of focus to let us really look at the warm, caring and creative sides of ourselves, and remember that this doesn't just mean eating, having families and staying warm, but being a whole person, being kind, compassionate, and protecting ourselves when necessary; being strong, but not too hard: the strongest trees bend in the storm, they don't break, so we celebrate that we can weather what life throws at us and come back stronger, just like the sun returning after the long winter sleep.

The Sun's Return

Orange streaking wonder like
Across the boards of blue
Calling unto you

Twanging every string
In the guitar of your soul
Alto cumulus
Herring backed and tickled pink
Perfect little lines
Framing the moon:
An absurdly gorgeous half
Smooth and sharply cut
A wedge of light
The opener
Before the main event.
The globe of yellow honey
Melting on the marshmallows
Of soft and drowsy clouds
Still awakening,
And gently gliding aside
Until gentle no more
The show hits the floor
The light, the bright, the glory ending night;
Sunrise.

The next big celebration is Beltane, the lead up to summer; May Day, when the hawthorn is in bloom and the sweet, pungent smell promises hot, sticky days to come. Fires are lit which have (or had) the dual purpose of encouraging the sun's progress towards midsummer, and also to kill any ticks, lice or other parasites that may now be plaguing the livestock with the return of the warmer weather. My Dad taught me that people would often dance or leap over the fire too – and often this was as much about de-licing as it was about fun and festivity! We believe, and I have no idea if this is universal among people who follow Celtic traditions, that the veil is thin at this time, just as it is at Samhain, which is pretty close to the opposite side of the year if you look at it as a wheel.

What does this mean? Well, the veil is a widely used term among Pagans (and others who follow a magical path) which refers to the barrier between what we see, laughingly referred to as the real world, and that which is otherworldly; spirits, the dead, ghosts, gods, ancestors, fairies, the fae or the sídhe. Is the veil truly a substantial wall which deteriorates at certain times of the year? I can't say, but I prefer to think of it like this: Everything that *can* be, exists all around us all the time. We can't see it all the time, we'd go mad. It would be simply *too much* input. So our brains, on a day-to-day basis, let us see and process pretty much only what we need to get through our day. Those of us who are attuned in some way to pick up things on what I can only call a different 'wave-length', may see more than others; some will receive this input all the time; others only when they try.

For some reason, perhaps because of centuries of belief and people practicing certain rituals at these key points during the year, there are times when seeing this other reality is easier; when we can see, hear and feel things around us that we would normally struggle to perceive. This, for me, is what is meant by the thinning of the veil, although as a spiritual experience it is very much open to debate! So, when the veil is thin or 'opens', magic then becomes easier. We are closer to our ancestors and give respect and honour to the deities/spirits that we feel close to.

As well as being a fire festival and a solar celebration, Beltane is traditionally a time to purify oneself, protect oneself from negative influences and basically get rid of any baggage you've been carrying unnecessarily. While we may not need to bound over fires to rid ourselves of parasites, in these modern (and thankfully more hygienic) times we leap the flames in joy and anticipation of the longest days to come. We think about our hardships, our concerns and our problems; as we take a deep breath and jump, we let go of our difficulties and the clamour of pain and grief. It all goes on the fire and you look forward to the height of summer with a light and happy heart.

From Lammas to Lughnasadh

August 1st is Lughnasadh, commonly accepted as a sort of first harvest festival. It literally translates as 'The Feast of Lugh' so no prizes for guessing who the primary deity involved here is. It originated as a funeral feast for Tailltiu, Lugh's beloved foster mother who sacrificed herself for her country.[16] It was a festival of games, feats of strength and also of peace and celebrating marriages – celebrating all that was good and happy about life.

It's approximately half way between the longest day, the summer solstice, and the autumn equinox, so essentially it's all about summer, heat, the height of good times and celebrating plenty. It just so happens to fall on the same date as Lammas, an Anglo-Saxon harvest festival which means 'loaf mass' and was a day to celebrate the first crops being brought in, often symbolised by baking a loaf from the first grain: traditionally barley, but of course now wheat is the grain of choice.[17]

So, as a 'modern Celt', what *am* I celebrating when I celebrate on this day? Do I continue seeking my Irish ancestors by examining only the Celtic festival of Lughnasadh, thereby ignoring my Anglo-Saxon heritage, or do I create some sort of hybrid of both? What do any of us do? Well I guess the real thing you have to look at is *why* we celebrate the turn of the seasons at all. Some might say that celebrating these quarter festivals helps keep you in touch with the seasons and reminds you that the world is turning, but my experience is that when you allow yourself to *feel* the turn of the seasons; the change of the weather and the growing and dying all around you; the creatures emerging from hibernation and the mating seasons and the foraging for food: this is what makes you *want* to celebrate. This is what gives you *reason* to celebrate.

Does it matter what the origin story of the name of the festival is? Does it matter what you call it at all? I asked my parents if they thought it was important to preserve the Celtic versions of the festivals, rather than simply celebrating because it feels natural to celebrate, depending on the season.

My Mum concurred that Lughnasadh, Beltane, Imbolc and Samhain are just names and you can call them whatever you feel like; the fact that they happen to have a Celtic name and some Celtic history attached to them isn't important. My Mum will even comfortably refer to Samhain as Halloween and we all happily indulge the practice of 'trick or treating' and acting like all the ghosts and ghoulies are out to getcha...

My Dad points out that the Celtic names are just linguistic remnants from history, fortunate enough to have such a strong mythological cycle built around them that they have lasted intact as a full calendar of events, but realistically these festivals will all have had many different names in many different places, in most cases prior to the appearance of the Celts. Lughnasadh was almost definitely Lammas first, and that was also the 'Gule of August,'[18] Gwyl Awst in Wales, and even just Harvest Home.

I love the idea that Lugh had this whole day, possibly a few days, dedicated to the woman he adored as his mother. But I also can't forget that the reason I *feel* like celebrating is because of the warm sun on my skin, food growing all around me and the heat of life literally buzzing to be appreciated. As Lugh is often recognised as a sun god, with his great shining face, I am sure he appreciates and approves of this too.

Day of the Dead

Samhain, for many on a Pagan-type path, is 'the biggy', the festival of all festivals, and much of this is to do with the day's association with the dead and thus ghosts, spirits and other things otherworldly. It's generally celebrated on October 31st although in Gaelic the word actually means 'November' so the festival being named thus would seem to indicate that it is to be celebrated at the start of November. This is probably because the Celts believed a new day started at sunset, so when fires were lit on the 31st October as the sun went down, it was already

Samhain, the next day, and time to celebrate another point in the year when the veil is thin and one can almost speak to one's ancestors, as they walk amongst us.

Sometimes the night-time celebrations are still called 'Samhain Eve' rather than Samhain, and I think it's key to understanding the Celts that we recognise that they weren't taken too much by the time of day or the date, but more by splitting things into light and dark. Sunset was the end of the current day; therefore it was the beginning of a new day. Samhain was the halfway point between equal night and day (the autumn equinox) and the longest night (the winter solstice). Winter was darker; summer was brighter.[19] This is how I believe they saw the world, and this is how, as someone trying to understand their ancestors, I am also finding myself looking at the world.

Even though we are, as a modern society, so obsessed with timekeeping and date stamping, it's nice just to think, 'It's cold and the sun is low after only a few hours, it must be winter. The moon is full and the sky is clear – it will be cold tonight. The leaves are yellowing; it is autumn.'

It's so much more special to watch the world change around you, to feel the turn of each season, than to mark its continuation by the flick of the page in a diary and waiting for dates to happen.

The most physical evidence of any sort of calendar kept by a Celtic people is the Coligny Calendar, bronze plates dating from around the year 200 (although it's thought the calendar usage may go back as far as 800 BCE) which show a calendar based on a five-year cycle using both the solar and lunar cycles to describe an approximately structured year. This is not unlike our modern Gregorian calendar if you think about it – we have months roughly based on the cycle of the moon, although as we only have 12 now we stick in random days here and there (i.e. the 30 and 31 day months). Every four years, when we've not managed to travel quite all the way around the sun, we get an extra day!

So here we are at Samhain. We now understand that the Celts

were looking forward into the darker part of the year and preparing for winter, while at the same time feeling the touch of the other world; the fae, the Tuatha Dé Danann and indeed their own ancestors.

Ever since I can remember this has always been a time to remember one's own ancestors and honour them the best you can. This can be simply saying their names out loud, or holding a feast with their favourite food included. A common practice is to leave an image out of the ancestor or ancestors in question, and if no image is available or appropriate then something that either belonged to them or reminds you keenly of them. This is their physical link to you; this is how they know where to come through when they reach the veil.

Offerings are left with this image or symbol, as a way of thanking your ancestor for what they have brought to you. Hopefully, your ancestor will see the gesture and be grateful, but also be at peace seeing that you are doing well and honouring your traditions; understanding yourself as a whole person, and acknowledging what came before you and what will come after. After all, by wholeheartedly embracing this practice you accept that one day you will be on the receiving end of the gesture – whether through a direct blood descendant or even from friends or students – anyone you may have had significant and positive influence on.

As well as honouring our ancestors, we also accept that in the long run, they no longer belong here. Not that they are unwanted, but that they now reside somewhere else, and only at Beltane and Samhain can we be this close to them again. Samhain, starting at sunset, has the longer darkness, and therefore the greatest opportunity to light fires and candles as beacons to guide the dead, which I think is why this winter festival is more widely recognised as the day of the dead, rather than its summer counterpart, which is more about the continuity of life and fertility.

So at Samhain, there tends to be a threefold celebration. We welcome the ancestors – we draw them towards us somehow, we feel their presence and we celebrate their return. We spend time among them, enjoying their company like you would a friend you have not seen for years. Not only ancestors but friends and acquaintances past, including pets and working animals that may have been close to us. It can be a very bitter sweet time of year: although it's wonderful to feel the presence of someone or something deeply missed, it also brings sharply into focus the original grief when you lost them.

Because of that though, it can be a great way of dealing with grief. Sometimes we bottle things up too much, and Samhain has a tendency to bring to the fore feelings we would not normally have to deal with on a daily basis. It's a good idea, because of this, to surround yourself with friends, family and loved ones or whoever can best support you through this. Of course, you may be someone who genuinely deals with grief better on your own, but when you are also dealing with the potentially supernatural, it's good to know that you are not alone; that you are not the only person who is feeling the presence of someone long gone but clearly not forgotten.

So this is the second stage of Samhain: being with those we lost, and dealing with it either with happiness or grief while ensuring we are supported and making it as joyous as possible with feasting, drinking, and even gifts. Some celebrate Samhain as New Year too (understandable looking at how the Coligny calendar split the year into two halves), so again, more drinking, gifts and excuses for tomfoolery!

The third stage is a little more solemn, and just as important. This is the stage where we feel the veil closing, and we say farewell to our ancestors (and other loved ones) and ensure we guide them on their way. There are many different ways of doing this and I would not recommend that you practice rituals, rites or magic with the intention of guiding the dead without the guidance of someone experienced in such matters – quite frankly it can be a bit scary. More simply and traditionally, candles can be lit as symbolic beacons to show the dead their paths. Music can be played, for in Celtic tradition music is a gift from the otherworld and thought to be very magical indeed. Ancestral feasts are cleared away and images of ancestors are cleaned and put away until after the season is over, to remove temptation for the spirit to stay. It's like saying, we've been happy to have you here, and we wanted to let you know how grateful we are for your influence in our lives. But we are the living; you are the dead. It's time for us to get back to our lives, and for you to return to whence you came.

I think it's very healthy in that way; we accept that our loved ones are gone. We in no way cling on to them or expect them to return to us to be a permanent part of our lives, and in this way we can deal with our grief and move on, although it can take several years for grief to lose its keen edge, of course. But we also accept that *here* is a time when we can celebrate them. Whether you believe that the dead physically (or metaphysically) return or not, how can anyone sneer at the idea of having a whole festival dedicated to love, remembrance and joy?

Hanging in the Balance

The Celts are renowned more for their celebration of the 'major' sabbats: Imbolc, Beltane, Lughnasadh and Samhain. Yet nowadays even those of us following a Celtic based tradition tend to celebrate the in-betweeners: the solstices and the equinoxes. They change slightly from year to year because their significance is based on where the earth is in relation to the sun, and of course, like the 'major' festivals, they are on different dates depending on where in the world you are.

In Britain, spring equinox is approximately 21st March, and autumn equinox around the 21st September. The equinoxes are moments of pure balance; day equals night; light equals dark.

Nothing outweighs the other; nothing has an advantage. Symbolic of peace, tranquillity and calm, but also the feeling of hanging in the balance, the calm before the storm; the moment where we pause, reflect and prepare, before sudden change, activity, bustle.

Think about the autumn equinox. Before supermarkets, cars and fridges, at this time of year people would have been racing to get ready for winter, knowing that the night is coming to swallow the light and bringing with it cold, frost, death and darkness. But, for now, we have a still point, a moment where we can gather ourselves, our resources and our energies and know that we are ready; ready for whatever the darker months may bring. We remember that they do not only bring the darkness without, but the hearth fires and joy within our homesteads, and that equally while we burn the fires to ward off the darkness, we accept the darkness as a vital part of the eternal cycle. We do not spit at it, hissing like a cornered cat; we prepare well and know that we are safe within our chosen havens – with family and loved ones to help out; with food and fire and knowledge that the sun is but a turn of the wheel away.

The spring equinox should be the same only in reverse, right? We all burst out of our houses to inhale the spring air and gather the bounty that surrounds us? Well, in theory, yes, but there's still an element of preparation and reflection. Imbolc has passed and hopefully we have sown the first seeds of our crops for the year, so it's time to plan what else must be done so that the coming warmer months can be enjoyed to their full.

At this time of year I do love so much to get out of the house, but in England often this is still a cold, rainy time and the 'promise' of spring on days like these truly has to be held in your heart! If the weather does let us down I like to make something – a cake, or some bread with something in it from last year's harvest, to remind me of the continuity of the world, the turning of the wheel, and that the rain and cold are just another part of springtime, and like all things, they will pass. Spring equinox is the closest festival to my birthday too, meaning it should stand out more for me, but really I don't see it as any more or less special than the other points in the year. It's magical because it's another time where the day does not challenge the night, and if times have been hard over winter now is the perfect time to find balance and hold it, become the pivot on the see saw – neither up, nor down, simply being, and appreciating that simple gift.

Summer solstice and winter solstice have always been very special for me (even before I began celebrating them formally) and it's hard to describe why. There is something powerful about knowing and understanding that the incredible, living rock you are a part of has reached a point where something is as much as it can be, and is poised, still for a moment, ready for everything to change.

I love it more, I think, because these festivals, like the equinoxes, are not based simply upon human observation and habits (like harvests and honouring the dead), but on simple (or incredibly complicated) astronomical physics. Whether we are here to observe and celebrate or not, the tilt of planet Earth means we will always have a longest day and a longest night in these parts of the world. The summer solstice should be the height of summer, but what I find interesting is that it's generally *after* the longest day (on or around the 21st June in the northern hemisphere) that we start to see the summer really kick in. Certainly in England, July and August are usually the hottest months, even though by this point the days have started short-ening.

I think this explains why the Celts were much more likely to have had their big celebration at Lughnasadh, the start of August, as the combination of heat and crops aplenty make for a great party! We tend to find that summer solstice is a mild, pleasant day, stretching into a long, golden sunset that we try to fill with family, friends, food and frolicking. We have had some wonderful big group picnics at this time of year, flying kites and playing games and really appreciating that *this is the most light we will ever have in one day* and it only happens, what, 75 to 100 times in your life? If you're lucky!

When you think of it like that, it makes you realise that these are the moments you need to cherish, to truly make the most of. I don't think I can remember a summer solstice where I've been stuck in the house doing nothing. Last year it rained but we all gathered at one house and feasted and laughed and when it dried out a bit we lit a fire and enjoyed the 'substitute sun', expressing gratitude for the things we make happen for each other, even when things don't go quite as planned. This year was spent with friends honouring the Morrigan and the fire within us all, and also doing my driving theory test – I got 100%, maybe that joy and appreciation for life does help out with mundane things as well...

And so we flip to the opposite side of the wheel. In Britain (amongst various other places), the winter solstice (on or around 21st December in the northern hemisphere) is sometimes also referred to as Yule, which has Germanic and Norse origins[20] and has sort of been absorbed into modern Paganism as part of the 'wheel of the year', although it has its own rich history and is celebrated worldwide in a myriad of different ways.

My most precious memories of the winter solstice all seem to be of going to a specific lakeside on the longest night. I remember it always feels later in the day than it is, because despite it only being early evening it is already pitch black, and once you move away from the roads there is only a little ambient light, depending on the weather and the moon.

One year, the black, velvet sky was perfectly clear, and the moon was completely full. The lake was frozen from one bank to the other, and glittered preciously in the cold blue light from above. Bare trees stretched their limbs in a perfect frame for this scene. There was no wind, and it seemed as if the world had been frozen into a perfect postcard simply entitled 'winter'. There were several of us together that year, and after our ritual celebrations we acted like children, walking out onto the ice and daring each other to go out a bit further, and pondering the strange shapes frozen within. It was simply a joyous time.

Another year in exactly the same place, the same group of us finished our celebrations, only to have a thick fog follow us all the way out to the path where we left the site. That was spooky, but exhilarating. We truly felt that whatever was abroad that night had said, 'Thanks, but it's time for you lot to go now: my turn'. We took the hint, I can tell you!

Another year we became a little lost in the dark, and weren't sure quite how to find the spot we were looking for. We heard wings overhead, and followed the sound. When the sound stopped, we checked our position. Shining our torches about, we discovered we had been led to the spot we had been searching for. As soon as we were done, a wind whipped up then suddenly stilled. Twigs snapped as though something heavy footed was walking towards us, and the wings began flapping back the way we came. We moved fast to follow the sound, and though the night had been still before, as we moved away from the woods and down the path, with the lake to our side, a new wind whipped ripples up across the surface of the water, seemingly always one step behind us. Just like the year before, we left swiftly and didn't look back.

Both these latter experiences led us to believe we had witnessed an aspect of 'The Wild Hunt': the idea that gods and their entourage, or in Celtic tradition the Fae or aos sí, ride out in a mad cavalcade to hunt down the unwary who dare to be abroad during the darkest midnight. We spent the rest of those evenings snug and warm, drinking and feasting and appreciating good company. Although we had a wonderful time and felt blessed to have felt that presence so strongly, we would not have ventured back there for anything less than an emergency.

So why are these turning points in the year so relevant in the 21st century? What does this structure mean to people who mostly deal with winter by putting the central heating on? How can celebrating the first harvest (whether you name it Lammas or Lughnasadh) hold any meaning for someone who buys their grain and flour at a supermarket, and therefore has it available all year round?

I can't answer for everybody, but for me personally, I love to feel connected to the world around me in some way. I already spoke of the joy of the warm, moist breath of spring upon my face; the sweet, earthy bite of autumn is no less fulfilling for me. So in part due to my Celtic ancestry and in part due to my own observations of this world, I will celebrate *all* eight of these turning points (any excuse for a good knees up!) as they each have their own unique significance. Each feast has an energy which if you pause and allow it, can flow through you, can be a part of you, and allow you to become a part of it, a part of the changing of the world, reminding us that nothing stays the same; we are always changing.

I am very conscious of the turning seasons, probably not quite in the same way my ancient ancestors were – not in a 'life or death' way, but in a way that lets me realise how the world around me works, and what would be happening just the same even if I were not here to witness and be a part of it.

As described earlier, it's a wet day today. I see people all around me heads down, just wanting to get out of the rain, and I feel grateful for having the sense to *be* grateful, to appreciate that this cool shower will start the plants shooting up in the garden, will start the turn of the wheel towards warmer, longer days. It's the beginning of another planting season, the beginning of another camping season and almost time for another equinox celebration; a time for work, pleasure and ritual.

So is this spirituality, or practicality? Well the Celts were renowned for both. The Romans are said to have been astonished by the range of gods and spirits they honoured, yet the Celts were feared for their prowess in war, helped mightily by their ability to travel far across land and sea.[21] So they were a practical people, who used their stories and legends as a way to record their exploits and, I suppose, spread fear and wonder at their apparently supernatural existence. Knowing the world, and how it turned, and how to live well in it whether through winter or summer, was a crucial part of this.

For me, it's a combination of both spirituality *and* practicality; having a balance between appreciating what's there and where it's taking you is one of the keys to finding balance within yourself and within your own life. Being closer to the earth, how it works, how things grow; this helps us understand that we have a responsibility towards it; it's not ours, but we are a part of it, and because we take so much from it, we really have to give something back!

I think some people find conflict between following a Pagan path and being part of modern society. Many of us lay claim to a harmony with nature and the earth, then drive miles and miles to get to some gathering or other, pumping out pollutants and notching up that ever present carbon footprint! I know very few people on any kind of Pagan path that are truly 'self sufficient' or living one hundred percent off the land without using any modern devices or techniques to help them in their daily lives. And there's no reason why they should be.

Having a connection to your ancestors is not about *becoming* your ancestors; having a connection to the world and nature is not necessarily about being a hermit. I think it's important to remember that everything really *is* about balance: using what you have, when you have to, and ensuring that any 'bad' behaviour is offset in some way.

Many people I know drive miles to get to farms, fields, woods and other venues for various events, yet most of those people are also deeply involved in the conservation of the area, the promotion of living spaces for local wildlife, the protection of natural woodland and hedgerows and the prevention of the destruction of natural habitats for the creatures that already reside there. So there is no spurning of modern society and very little hypocrisy, just a genuine desire to better understand the natural world, become a part of it rather than just living of it, and perhaps get a glimpse of life as it is without the trample of busy human feet.

Chapter Three

Magic – The Craft of the Fae

I've already spoken of my amazement at discovering a group that were as interested in the Celtic legends as I was, and the profound effect that had on me. There were other astounding discoveries to be made that I can't go into in too much detail for fear of breaking vows of privacy and bonds of friendship – a story told in confidence is a powerful binding! But let it just be said that I have been fortunate enough to discover that it's not just me who longs to open a doorway into these fantastic stories, legends, and whatever else one may name the Tuatha Dé Danann. So, how exactly does one do this? And how do they, as deities or spirits, lend themselves to magical workings?

Well firstly, I better explain what I mean by this. If you're reading this then hopefully you've got a vague idea that some people, including some Pagans, practise magic. Not all do and some will not refer to it as that, so please forgive me if I generalise. 'What is magic?' is yet another question, like the aforementioned 'What is a Pagan?' that gives multiple answers, all correct, all unique to the person you are asking and probably all contradictory to some extent! My own understanding is that magic is the science and understanding of the way things work.

'What things?' I hear you ask. Everything! When a tulip starts sprouting in the snow, somehow aware of the warm months ahead, this is magic. When the bus comes literally as I get to the stop, that's magic too. When I don't get a role at work that I wanted but this means I have more time to work towards a different endeavour, this is also magic.

'That's not magic, that's just things happening! Normal things!' I hear you cry. Oh yes. Magic is normal. Magic is everyday events. Magic is the world changing around us, just outside our control, but close enough to appear mundane.

My definition of *practising* magic, using it as a tool, is that you move that little bit closer to the world and you *take control*. Although it is a skill, some people manage this without any conscious effort. Those who always get the job they want, or win £10 on scratch-cards weekly; you all know someone like this: an individual who seems incessantly lucky. I think it works the other way too; I'm sure that those people who always seem down on their luck and always seem to be carrying burdens or personal tragedy; I think perhaps they are also closely connected to the world but for whatever reason they attract the wrong sort of events. I have no idea how this works, it's just an approximate theory, and a hair's breadth away from total digression, so let's continue on...

To summarise, when you do a magical working, you have a goal in mind (hopefully!) and you do something in order to make it happen; to partially or completely take control of events. Sometimes this may be as simple as wanting to feel a connection to something; a god, a spirit, the energy involved with the change of season; it may also be a specific or complex task such as healing someone or looking for answers. I refer to this practice as witchcraft, and in this bracket I include herbalism, making incense, writing music (powerful music anyway, music that moves someone in some way) and pretty much anything that involves changing the world in some way, however small.

Most witches I have met deal primarily with people, and usually practise healing of some sort. There's no way to say 'how' to do this without giving a context because absolutely everyone will do things differently. I know people who will spend days working with a specific deity to help someone through a time of illness, and others who seem to be able to reassure and bolster another's spirit with but a thought. Some work in groups, some work alone. Some do a combination of both. Some will use magic as part of a religious experience while others will see it as a purely practical thing. Some actually refer to witchcraft as a religion, while others combine witchcraft and other magic with totally separate religions or practices. The specific context isn't massively important for this basic understanding, and if you want to know how to practise magic, then it's best to find some one-on-one guidance. I don't really believe you *can* learn magic entirely from books, although books can certainly help you down a path towards finding magic in your own life. So we return to the question. How can the Tuatha Dé Danann lend themselves to magical workings? How can these Celtic legends, these deities or spirits that have survived millennia, be relevant to the witches of today?

For me, the main relevance is that when I practise magic, I'm in some way reaching into the universe, or the bits of the world I can't see, and trying to make a change in some way. Legend states that the Tuatha Dé Danann, at their end, didn't die, but moved aside for the new people, and disappeared into an invisible realm, always around us, but just out of sight, and out of reach.

We're the mystery of the lake when the water's still.
We're the laughter in the twilight
You can hear behind the hill.
We'll stay around to watch you laugh,
Destroy yourselves for fun.
But, you won't see us; we've grown sideways to the sun.[22]

These beings were powerful, and magical, yet knew their time in the corporeal world was up, so they changed themselves; to still be in the world, they drifted aside, to leave their magic and mystery as a reflection of their former glory. This was a bid for immortality, insurance that they would never really end, and I am sure, like others who have experienced a connection to the Tuatha Dé Danann, that they were successful!

There are plenty of examples of the magic and spells woven by these beings, with a big focus on shapeshifting and other transformations like causing people to sleep, or casting compulsions upon one another. One such powerful compulsion is a geas, such as the one on Cú Chulainn which means he may never eat dog meat, because the dog is his totem animal – he is the Hound of Ulster. However, he is also compelled, possibly through another geas, possibly via the general laws of courtesy at the time, to accept any meal offered to him. You can see where this is going right? Of course his enemies figure this out and he is brought down low by being offered dog meat to eat, ouch.[23]

I think this is a really strong story to deliver the lesson many of us have to learn the hard way – magic is *dangerous*. You may think you want to change the world, or yourself, but have you *really* thought it through? Are you absolutely sure that there are no possible consequences? If there are, then will you be a hundred percent ready to accept and deal with them? Cú Chulainn was pretty unlucky and, of course, not many of us will end up strapped to a stone dying because of a curse. I hope.

But there are things you have to remember about magic; you have to take responsibility, not just for your actions, but for your intentions. You have to be utterly committed to what you are doing, and know what you are doing – dithering is not the magical way forward. And most of all, if it's not necessary, don't do it. Your friend may ask you to do a spell to help them get a job. Well, you could absolutely do that. You could ask for dreams to come to you for guidance; you could cast herbs into the wind; you could summon your ancestors and ask them to give your friend strength and confidence.

But how about you go round, sit down together and make a list of potential interview questions? Or help them build a CV? Honestly, these things are also magical in their own way – magic really, really doesn't need to come from the hidden realms – a basic task can have a much more profound effect. A simple meal felled one of Ireland's greatest heroes. A kind thought put into action can be just as powerful.

The Power of Prophecy

Throughout the Celtic legends there are references to prophecies, futures foretold and promises made by victors and losers alike. One of the most famous prophecies by the Morrigan is told at the end of Cath Maige Tuired, the great battle that Lugh wins against the Fomorians, and is conflicting at best. Elizabeth Gray's translation tells us that the first section prophecies a time of fullness and peace, but then the Morrigan goes on to foretell doom, betrayal, and the end of the world.[24]

In Táin Bó Cúailnge, Queen Medb demands a poetess to divine the fate of her army in the upcoming battle against the Ulster men. The prophetess does as she is told, but Medb is not happy. She discovers, although she does not believe it, that her army will be greatly reduced by the power of one young man.

Prophecy of this kind is indeed a double edged sword; sometimes simply hearing the prophecy can be the spark that makes it come true, and sometimes doing everything one can to avoid the outcome of the prophecy can cut the very rut that holds the wheels of fate. Medb, in a way, does exactly what she should do, which is to ignore the prophecy and carry on towards the battlefield, but in this case the prophecy is not self-fulfilling (meaning she could potentially have changed events by listening to the prophecy), and Cú Chulainn is indeed the young lad who will see the host blood-stained and red.[25]

So what should Medb have done? Taken her army home? What do we do, when faced with the promise of failure? Do we give up? Or do we fight in the face of adversity? Well, each of us will have our own answer for that, and I for one know there have been times when I knew that continuing to fight was *not* the best course of action, and indeed sometimes backing down, though it may hurt the pride and ego, will be less painful in the long run.

Telling the future is something we do every day without realising it. We plan our week, or our month, and even the years ahead. Although we can't predict extraordinary events, such as natural disasters or sudden illness, we can safely say some things are fairly certain. I know that tomorrow I'll be getting up and going to the office, and that my son will be at his grandparents, and that we'll eat dinner in the evening. I can even foretell that, knowing me, I'll probably stay up too late either writing or reading, and have a groggy head first thing on Thursday morning! This is not magic as such; it is simply recording and replaying the events that have gone before, and understanding the characters in the theatre of one's life; knowledge which allows us to, within a certain degree of accuracy, foretell what will happen to us over a period of time.

So what do we do when we either need more detail than this, or need to look into something with which we have no or little experience? This would be the kind of prophecy I would call magic, although the best 'fortune tellers' I have found are those who are simply incredibly adept at reading people and under-standing their reactions to particular situations. I say 'simply', however this word does not convey the incredible amounts of respect I have for someone who is able to do this; to be able to look at someone and from their body language, replies and reactions discern an entire personality, and from that give guidance and suggestions to a probable outcome to any given situation. That, to me, is a real power, real magic, and certainly not to be sneered at.

Of course there are charlatans, and if anyone ever started a 'reading' for me by talking about a tall, dark stranger I would walk out in no short order! But I certainly know that when needing guidance it's not uncommon for people to turn to different forms of prophecy, including fortune telling, readings from cards (such as, but not limited to, tarot) and other forms of divination, to try to get a glimpse into their future.

Does it help? Does having guidance as to what may be around the corner actually aid us in any way? Or is it better to deal with things as and when they happen; to react to each situation without any forethought other than that which is given to us by everyday events?

I spoke to my friend Emma, who is unusual in that she experiences what can only be described as premonitions. For most of her life she has felt changes in herself and her own moods whenever something has been pending either in her life or the lives of those close to her or connected to her, but she has little or no control over it. We got together to chat about her unique situation.

I ask her to try to describe what it's like when she feels something and then that feeling is subsequently followed by an event or occurrence. I immediately realise I am massively simplifying this for Emma; as this conversation progresses, you will see what I mean. This level of connection to a prophetic talent is so subtle yet enormous at the same time, it's difficult to describe, and having only ever had prophetic dreams myself, and not very often, it's a feeling I can only experience as an outsider looking in.

Emma is thoughtful as I ask her to give me some examples of when this has happened to her, and I feel like I am asking her to use finger paints to show me the Mona Lisa. We talk about the differences between large and small events, and I ask her to try to describe just how it affects her everyday life. She gives a few examples such as having a strong feeling she should not go out on a particular night, but ends up going out anyway; ends up regretting it due to personal situations that arise. I postulate that perhaps it is prior experience that gives her this warning; Emma counters by saying everyone has the ability to listen to their inner voice, the voice of premonition, but for some reason Emma's is louder, and it's *because* of her prior experiences with the premonitions and these feelings, that she listens to the messages she is being sent. Or not, at times! This leads to the situations where she admits she regrets having gone against her own instinct.

'In general I'm aware that it's happening; I'm aware that it [the premonition] is there and I'm feeling a certain way. I just choose whether to act on it or not. Most of the time there's absolutely no point because I never know what it's for anyway. Like when I found out about my friend being ill. I had the feelings for ages before then and I knew it was something; it was building up and up and up every day, and then it stopped. A few days later, he rang me, and the day that it stopped was the day he'd been to the doctor's and found out just how ill he was. So I just think it's bloody pointless, because I've no idea what it's for, so there isn't anything I can do with it. If you don't know what it's about, what are you supposed to do? So for that reason I don't even see the point in me getting these feelings.'

This sense of frustration is overwhelming – the knowledge that something, either your own talent, or something supernatural, is trying to give you a warning about something, but not quite giving you enough information to do anything other than feel anxious and wonder what is going to happen next.

Emma describes the physical feeling: 'It's like when you see somebody you fancy. My tummy goes funny, and my legs go really weak. It's like, when people say you've got butterflies, but it's not; it's different but it's hard to explain how it's different. I can tell the difference between just being nervous and having my feelings.'

I say this sounds like an intense feeling of anticipation.

Emma agrees to a certain extent: 'Yes. But you never know if it's something you should be excited about, or worried about, and I can't do anything or concentrate on anything when it's happening, because I'm so aware that it's there, and because I don't have any clue whatsoever what it relates to. You're just constantly worrying about what it might be or who it might be, even though you know eventually you'll find out. I couldn't stop it [the event], because I don't know what it is.

'I always think that when people talk about prophecy, what other reason is there for knowing what's going to happen, than to be able to prepare for it and maybe do something about it? But the trouble is, to do that, you need to know what it is that's coming, and I don't have that. It's kind of like the whole 'fight or flight' thing you're meant to get; it's like I get that without knowing why. So in some ways it's like I'm waiting for something. I kind of get myself ready, but I've no idea what it's for.'

I try and imagine the horrific stress of trying to prepare yourself for anything; knowing, with complete certainty, that the feeling you are having means something is about to happen, but having no idea what it may be. I ask Emma how she copes with the stress.

'I just get really angry; if it is something bad happening to somebody I care about, I just get so angry afterwards with myself and then I end up shouting at whoever it might be that's doing it, or whatever's doing it, because I couldn't help them. I couldn't do anything to stop it and I can't do anything to change it, so why can't I just be like everyone else where it's totally out of the blue they get this news? Whereas I've been sat there waiting for whatever it was that's coming. P*sses me off!'

I think this is the worst aspect of this; knowing you probably couldn't have done anything about it anyway. Even if Emma had known, with certainty, that the stressful feelings she was having were about her sick friend, what could she have done to prevent that sickness? How many others have had a strange feeling when they are about to lose a loved one or receive bad news, but really, what can we do about this? Is it just a form of preparation?

My friend Chris told me about the passing of the mother of his wife, Fi. When he contacted his own mother to relay the tragic news, she said, 'So that's who it was'. Again, she had felt something, a disturbance or a great sadness, but had not known what or who it related to. I wonder, out loud, if this aspect of Emma's nature has ever worked to her advantage in any way.

She replies: 'If there's somebody I want to avoid, I can go out and know that I'm safe to go out; they're not going to be there. Then there's other times I think I won't. It's like you get that kind of feeling that you know something's coming, but because I know what's happening in certain situations I can kind of narrow it down to the fact that whoever it is, is going to be there.'

So Emma here is using this feeling, this sense of premonition, combined with her everyday knowledge of what is going on right now in her life, the choices laid out before her and the 'cast of characters' involved to narrow the possibilities down, and often she is right, saving herself some potential embarrassments or confrontations, and also occasionally giving her a bit of freedom and relaxation for the times when she feels she can go into situations knowing she *won't* be walking into trouble. I wonder if there have ever been times when she has completely changed her plans because of these feelings, or simply stayed in the house.

'Yes,' she says. 'Sometimes I get it and it's not even like my funny feelings, more like just something that says, 'I know I shouldn't go out tonight', not like last night [the regretted night out], but where I feel I really, really shouldn't go; something is *telling* me not to go out.

'Then there's always some big drama and something happens, generally bad. I don't really ever get that feeling, then go out and have a really good time. I still nearly always go out though, because I don't trust it. With the funny feelings, I don't want to trust it, but I've never been wrong. I've had them, then they've stopped, like I was saying about my friend; it seemed nothing had [apparently] happened, then all of a sudden I'll find out that something did happen. And as soon as whatever it is happens, the feelings stop. It's literally like a switch; it just goes straight away. Even though I've always had some kind of evidence after-wards that the feelings were telling me something, I still can't trust it. I wouldn't do anything. You can't live like that.

'When I have it [the feeling] I'm just sat waiting for something bad to happen. As soon as I get it – my Mum knows all about this; I'll ring her up and say, 'Have you spoken to my sisters', and she'll know straight away. She'll ask me, 'Have you got your funny feelings?' I'll say yeah and she's like, 'I'll ring them'.

'When Granddad died I was getting them for ages, and he'd been ill but he was alright then, and then he had another stroke and for about three or four days before I was saying, 'I'm having my funny feelings Mum,' and we were kind of joking saying, 'Ooh, god I hope it's not me.' Then we got the phone call about granddad. My Mum just looked at me; I think it scares some people, but I think that's just because of a lot of things that have happened in our family. If that wasn't the case I might get more excited, because usually things happening out of the blue, they're either really bad or really good things aren't they? But I'm just used to them being really bad. If that was rare I'd probably get more excited. I think I'd look at the whole thing completely differently. I'd see it as a good thing.'

I wonder, on the back of this comment, if it has ever *been* a good thing. Emma confirms she had the feelings for two weeks or so before she got the call to say she had been given a role on the Sweeney Todd film. I wonder if that is just the combination of stress, anxiety and anticipation – waiting to hear about an important job can create all sorts of inner turmoil!

Emma explains: 'I didn't audition for it: I didn't know anything about it. My agent got the casting call, and my agent's assistant sent my photo off. That was two weeks before, probably around the same day I started getting the feelings, although I don't know exactly what date that was. So it was totally out of the blue for me; I had no idea the film was even being made at that point. I had no idea. Sometimes even if it's just that I get an audition: you know last week when I had a couple? I woke up and I had the feelings, but for some reason I wasn't getting stressed about them, I just kind of had them and, maybe because I was tired, just ignored them. Then I got the text to ring my agent later that day about an audition, and he had put me in for it that morning.'

This, to me, is the clearest example that the 'gift', if I can call it such a name, that Emma, and others like her have, seems to be connected directly to the events occurring around her without her other senses i.e. sight, sound, even memory, getting involved at all. It's as if a part of her brain is out there, scanning the world for potential events that might affect her in the future, and then causing some sort of chemical imbalance, creating these feelings that let her know *something*, whether good or bad, is on its way. I comment on how accurate the timings seems to be, that from what Emma is saying, the dates she starts to have those feelings, are the start dates of the events, or the triggers leading up to the events.

She says: 'I write it down in my diary which is how I can work out the dates later on. But if I haven't written in my diary for a while then I don't remember because it [the feeling] is pretty common. But if I go about two or three weeks without getting them, I think that's when I start getting really bored and really fed up. I've not had my funny feelings, so I just presume nothing's coming; everything's going to stay exactly the same. You know when you get these phone calls from me saying, 'I'm bored, I'm fed up, nothing's going on', which is what I was like the other week, then I woke up with the feelings and now I've been auditioning and stuff.

'Things have started happening again. When I don't get them, I get maybe just as, well, not stressed but; even though a lot of the time it ends up being bad things, if I don't have them, I feel like there's no chance of something good happening either, so I get quite disappointed if I haven't had them for a while.'

I guess this is the trade off – if you want exciting things to be happening in your life, you have to take the rough with the smooth, and of course this is the same for everybody. But when your whole body, your whole being, makes every effort to keep you updated with what might be around the corner, how can you cope knowing that, while nothing bad might be happening, also there may be nothing good, joyful, exhilarating or inspiring either? I wonder if anything surprising has occurred out of the blue for Emma, without her experiencing the feeling beforehand. Has she ever been taken completely by surprise?

'No. Honestly, totally honestly, no. There might have been times where I've been surprised because they weren't that strong, but I've never *not* had them. Even silly things like that night we went out near Christmas and a certain person turned up; seeing someone I've not seen for a while, or someone I like, I get the feelings before things like that happen. A lot of the time, for example with another person in particular, I went six months without seeing them, then I started getting my funny feelings and having dreams about them – so sometimes I have *dreams* about them as well – then I end up seeing them out of the blue.

'I remember when me and an ex broke up the first time; we weren't talking at all, apart from the odd, angry text about who would get the TV stand, you know, things like that. We broke up in the summer and I'd say up to winter we didn't speak at all. All of a sudden I started getting my funny feelings and I had dreams about him – he kept popping up in my dreams and I kind of just chose to ignore it because I thought well, we just broke up, I'm not going to totally forget about him, maybe it's just he's still in there and I'm ignoring it.

'It happened for about a week and the first night he was just in the background of the dream, then the second night he was having conversations with people in the dream and as the nights went on he got nearer to me and nearer to me and him having a conversation. In the last one, and this is in my diary so I can prove this; I had a dream that it was near Christmas and that I was at what I thought was a sauna, because there was lots of wood on the walls in this room. We got back together; he told me that he wanted to be with me. I remember waking up thinking, 'That was weird.' I'd been up about five minutes; I was still kind of laid in bed thinking about my dream, when my phone went and it was him. He asked me to go meet him for a drink. We ended up spending the whole day together, and nothing further happened, but I'd had the funny feelings and the dream so I wasn't surprised.

'Later, it was just after Christmas; so between Christmas and New Year, and we were having a party at a friend's house. It was the first time I'd been, and in the living room, it was all wooden panels on the walls. My ex wasn't there; he was away, but I was in that room when he rang me and told me how he felt about me, so sometime the dreams do link in with my feelings.'

I comment that the details from the dream, while not an accurate rendition of how things occurred, were pretty specific.

Emma says: 'Well I've had a few like that. My sister got with her husband when I was 17 so I'd have been 15 when this happened. I had a dream, and this is in my dream journal, so I can show you this one as well. I dreamt she had a little girl, who was really, really tiny, she was really small, and she had loads of black hair. I remember even in my dream thinking that was weird because we're all blond. She was called Charlotte. I remember telling my sister about it and she was like, 'Yeah right', and didn't pay any attention to me. I told my Mum and they all just went, 'OK, whatever', but it kind of stuck with me, that dream.

'Then what, seven years later my sister had a little girl called Charlotte, who was really premature and really small. She was in hospital for a long time. She had loads of dark hair – she's really blond now but she had loads and loads of black hair. I was like, 'Told you!' and my sister was like, 'What you on about?' Because she didn't remember any of it. So yeah, sometimes I have pretty specific dreams. Like the bombings in London. I had a dream; I woke up that morning and I was at work at 9am, and I could walk to work so I didn't have to get the tube or anything, but that night I'd had a dream about being in a tunnel with some people and we could hear – I can't remember if it was an explosion or more like a crash; it was that kind of loud, impact sound. I was trying to tell everyone, 'Get out of here!' and they were like, 'We can't, we've got to get to work', and I was like, 'You've gotta get out! You've gotta get out!'

'I woke up, and it was a really weird dream, really vivid, and went to work and my friend was there, and you know when you have weird dreams, you tell them people about them don't you? I told her my dream, and she was like, 'You have weird dreams!' and we were just talking about it. Then our manager came running in and he said, 'Emma, do you know where your boyfriend is?' I was like, 'He's in bed, why?' and he said, 'Have you not heard what's happened?' Then he told us about the bombs on the tubes and the friend I had told about the dream couldn't talk to me for about a week after; she was terrified of me. It was the fact I had told her before it had happened; if I'd told her after it had happened she'd have been like, 'Whatever'. So sometimes things that I'm not actually really involved in do pop up.'

Dreams are certainly an interesting aspect of prophecy. Stories of dreams that foretell events to come are incredibly popular and seem to be some of the longest lived of our ancient tales. A fantastic example from Wales is the Dream of Macsen Wledig – not a Celt at all but a Roman conqueror. There are echoes of this story in the Celtic tale of Óengus, who like Macsen, dreams of a woman he falls in love with, and he is so convinced of the truth of his dream that his mother, Boann, searches Ireland for a year; his father, the Dagda, does the same, then she is found in a cave by the lake of the Dragon's mouth held captive with dozens of other girls, except the girls were all in the form of birds, including his potential love.[26]

Transformation, things hidden and confusion; how many of

us have had dreams like this? Dreams where we are simply not sure what *is* real and what is fantasy; which scene is taken from our day-to-day lives and which is utterly fabricated by our insatiable imagination? Emma's dreams that she describes above show that the scene is often played out in ways we can't possibly decipher until after the events have happened, which makes it difficult to use dreams as any sort of tool. I mentioned earlier that I sometimes have prophetic dreams, which sounds very mystical but honestly, it's pretty useless – at best entertaining and illuminating, at worst confusing and upsetting.

I'll give you an example of the former: this was a very strange dream. The night began outside an enormous tree with an incredibly wide trunk and wide spreading branches, like a horse chestnut. It's strange that I didn't see the leaf type because I love trees and would have recognised the species, but I didn't remember when I awoke what kind of tree it was. A great door in the trunk led up some stairs then out again to a balcony that ran all around the outside of the tree. Half the circumference had a bar (a bar you drink at, with a bar man – told you it was strange!) nestled into the tree itself, and it was very cramped getting past the crush of people on the narrow balcony. At the end of the bar was a small stage, and my friend Emma began to sing with somebody, but I could not remember who it was. I knew we had seen somebody from a band we knew, but this wasn't the person she was singing with. We had a great time, and although the dream continued I couldn't remember much after this.

I told Emma about the dream the next day, via a text message. I was a bit stunned when she texted me back to say she had been out with the people in question that night, mostly with the person I had seen her on stage with. With regards to the singing, well, she might just be appearing in a music video. We laughed about the coincidence, and then a few days later I got another text telling me what the band's logo was – a tree. I was astounded. What's baffling is that the dream is almost pointless. I basically, through a mish-mash of symbol and situation, documented what was happening in my friend's life at the time, even though I hadn't seen her and was only finding out the actual events a few days later.

At the time we hypothesised it was maybe just because we were so close, that I was linking into her when I was at rest and she was still busy – it was not long after my son was born so I was napping as much as possible and getting early nights where I could! So maybe my subconscious brain was tapping into her more active brainwaves and giving me a distorted but enter-taining review of events. Other things like that happened too; I would dream about her in a particular situation, and it would turn out that was what was happing in the book she was reading before she went to bed, again backing up the theory that my resting mind was tapping into what her active mind was doing. We wondered if this happened because of Emma's affinity for premonition combined with my forays into witchcraft, but we never really got an answer and it stopped happening so frequently when I returned to work; probably too much stress for my mind to relax entirely the way it was when I was just at home with the family.

I've started writing these dreams down, and I would definitely recommend anybody interested in their dreams to do the same, if only to try to notice any patterns in the dreams, and to document instances when things that happen in your dreams seem to parallel events in real life; perhaps not in your own experiences, but in those of someone you are close to. At first you end up writing every dream down, which is good as it trains you to remember as much detail as you can, but I have found that as I have progressed with this practice I can pretty much pick out which are the significant dreams. As soon as I wake I reach for my phone and tap the rough points into my notepad, then try to flesh it out so I keep as much detail as possible. Some of these I will look back on and think, wow, great dream, utter nonsense though! Others I can see as either slightly prophetic, scrying, or catalytic; the dream either tells me something is coming, let's me peep at something that is already happening, or prompts a change in my life by me following a message I have been given by my subconscious. Whether I am alone in that subconscious or guided by another is another question entirely.

Healing Hands

So many Celtic legends have supernatural healing woven into them it is hard to know where to begin! Sometimes one character heals another, often after wounding them in the first place, such as when Cú Chulainn blesses and restores the Morrigan as thanks for quenching his thirst, after he smote her three times when she was in the form of an eel, then a wolf, and finally a heifer.[27] You've already seen the excerpt from 'How the Dagda got his Magic Staff' where the Dagda is almost shamed into restoring his victims back to life with his newly acquired magic staff or club.

I think in all cultures the idea of healing someone is magical and anyone who could heal would be treated with reverence and in some cases even fear. After all, that which we do not understand is often the most fearful, and perhaps those who can give life can also take it away? Author and healer Gina McGarry tells us that the Celtic physicians employed pure water, fresh air and cleanliness as allies in the healing process,[28] things that seem obvious to us now but that over the millennia since the Celts were in Britain and Europe, clearly have not always been at the forefront of medical practice. It's only in the past few hundred years that in Britain, we discovered that perhaps throwing our bodily waste out into the streets was not an amazing idea after all.

The Celts seem to also have been fond of tales that describe healing implements, tools that are imbued with the magic property of healing. We've already looked at the Dagda's club and cauldron, both restoring and life bringing. Then there's poor

Cían's blood price, chosen by Lugh, including apples from the garden in the east of the world, which taste of honey and remove the pain of wounds and all sickness. One of these apples a day would definitely keep the doctor away! The second item he asks for is also a healing item (unsurprising I suppose, he was just about to go to war) which is the pig skin of Tuis (a king in Greece) which heals any wound and any sickness. Again with the pigs; he also wants seven pigs which are apparently immortal and can be eaten over and over and the eater will never suffer from any disease or sickness.[29]

These miraculous items may have existed, but is more likely that the druid or wise person who employed them was simply exceedingly skilled at herbalism and psychology, and knew the best ways to heal people with the materials available. Saying you have a magic pig skin? Means people won't think too much about the brew you are giving them, or the herbs you are putting in a poultice, and makes it less likely for others to figure out your skills, giving you a unique edge and a revered position in society.

Healers today range from doctors and nurses at your local surgery or health centre to brain surgeons to acupuncturists to crystal healers to homeopaths to herbalists. There are so many different paths to helping others heal. Some require tools, some don't. All require skill and training of different levels depending upon what is required. My mother in law performs Reiki, which is a method of healing that she describes as a non-invasive therapy using universal energy. I ask her to tell me a bit about how she developed her skills, and how it works, and begin by asking her what drew her to healing others.

Cath's Experience

Why does it appeal to me? Simply because it gives me the oppor-tunity to help someone else, someone who is in need. Helping to heal others helps me to connect with everything and everyone. It reminds me that everything in the world is connected in some way to every-thing else. I feel an awesome connection to the universe which you could describe as a connection to God. Reiki is love and the universe is love, so I am blessed to give and receive unconditional love.

I should tell you that Reiki tends to choose the person; most of the holistic therapies I do that help or heal in some way have some form of Reiki in. I do reflexology [a therapy involving applying pressure to zones or reflex areas that correspond to different areas of the body, with the goal of causing change or healing in that area of the body] on people's feet and even while doing this there may be aspects of Reiki involved. If I give an Indian head massage, or even a Swedish massage, elements of Reiki are in there.

To develop your skills as a healer is just like developing your skills in anything else; it takes practice! Also you must go through training. Reiki has a scale of ability: Reiki 1 is beginner level, Reiki 2 is intermediate, and these two levels can be achieved in anything between six and 18 months depending on the person. Reiki 3 is Master level. It can take another three or four years after the Reiki 2 level has been achieved, again depending on the person. Some people will get there sooner, and others take longer. At this stage you learn to be able to teach the skills to others, and to attune others [an experience sometimes described as an initiation into the healing universal energy] if you so wish. Personally I am not drawn to teaching. I have only been a master for three or four years; I am still a very young master!

I don't see myself as healing anyone. I am simply a channel for the universal energy. It is this energy that provides the healing. It's safe to say that everyone has the capacity to be a channel for healing, just as everyone has the capacity to be a channel for Spirit. Everyone is born with gifts and talent; some of us know what we have been blessed with from an early age; others (like myself) don't realise our full potential until adulthood.

Cath is skilled in many different types of massage and is learning more all the time. She is very modest about her skills, and although she can be rewarded for them she doesn't make a living off them, like a Celtic healer would have been able to do. I think this is one aspect of modern society where the fact that we veer away from our ancestors is unfortunate; we no longer honour those who bring healing, because so many of us are empowered to heal ourselves.

In fact, we are actively encouraged by the government and NHS not to bother doctors with our ailments but to go online and check our symptoms, and to self-medicate and only seek professional advice if our own ministrations fail. I think it's a good idea, a *great* idea to know our own bodies well, including how to help ourselves, but when there is someone in the community who can benefit everyone with their healing knowledge and skill, I think it would be great to put those people on a bit of a pedestal, and ensure the community looks after them.

In some ways, looking after one's self and healing one's self, instead of someone else, can be the hardest thing to do. Physical healing throws up obvious difficulties, because when you are sick or in pain, you find it harder to focus on what you are doing and may not have the strength or dexterity for what is required. Mental or psychological healing; well, the fact that this is required shows that one is perhaps not in the state of mind one needs to be in, in order to create the kind of space for the healing 'magic' to work in. Sometimes simple changes of perspective can be enough. I'll give you an example, along the topic of forgiveness.

Sometimes I really struggle with being a forgiving person. In my formative years, I was a bit of a doormat and gave people chance after chance, even after they had let me down multiple times – sometimes regarding promises made and broken, sometimes regarding matters of the heart; sometimes simply in practical matters like money or housing. Unfortunately some of those people, now no longer in my life, did not deserve those chances, and I have now learned to not be so accommodating.

The scar this has left is that I have a tendency to feel hard done by as soon as anyone 'wrongs' me. Sometimes I'm so keen to defend myself and be sure I'm not taken advantage of, that I see slights where none are intended; I feel pain at the slightest knock to my ego, and sometimes I really don't see the funny side of what turns out to be genuine banter. Worse still, sometimes I try to hold people accountable for what turns out to be a genuine mistake or error on their part; the true knife is in the intent, and if there is no intent, how can there be a wound? Of course one can hurt others unintentionally, but kind words and apologies are time-honoured remedies for this ill. And this is where forgiveness comes in.

My change of perspective, my *healing*, is that I need to hone the art of recognising when someone is genuine about their mistake, and make room inside for that little warm spot that swallows the hurt and transforms it, absorbs it; dissolves it with laughter, embarrassment or simply a kind word. Because the forgiveness not only reassures the instigator; it cools the fires within the one who got burned (me in this example), divesting them of anger and making for a brighter, happier day.

My Dad always said that lower magic is changing things around you, but higher magic is changing things within yourself. Now that's not everybody's definition, but it certainly explains why it's so hard to make a change within yourself, even when you can see easily what the person next to you would need to do in order to achieve the same goal.

The Witchcraft of Craft

The sun rises; the sun sets.
It is another day.
Another path to tread,

To leave footprints in the dirt.
Or to pass unnoticed.
Counting only seconds
Only minutes
Held not within the turn of the earth
But trapped within the turn of the clock.
When sirens speak
To start your day
With clamour abhorrent
While you still lay
Clinging to dreams and wishes and fear;
Then rise and wake and listen.
Not because the alarm tells you to;
Not because it is routine;
Not because you follow another
But simply so at the end of another day
You may turn behind
And see with pride
The footprints left firmly marked
Where you have walked.

How many of us do this; walk each day knowing we have made an impact in some small way? And how do we empower ourselves to do that? Well, most of us do it by having a particular skill. Not a magical skill; not in the most common understanding of the word 'magic', but a normal, everyday skill that we hone until it is ours, and ours alone.

What do I mean by this? Well, I have a friend who does beautiful jewellery. Every time I see her post a picture online of one of her new creations, I know that whatever else has happened that day, she will go to bed knowing she has created something beautiful that will bring someone, even if it's only herself, a piece of happiness. I have another friend who studies fragrances, smells and cleaning products to make the most amazing toiletries. She truly is an alchemist, and again, even though she has been crafting for a long time, I know she is always trying to improve and create new items, so the passion to stretch herself keeps her inspired.

So why is this magic? Well firstly, for me, it's the unique nature of the craft. The crafter takes a fairly generic skill to start with, and then makes it their own, so that anyone who sees the work will know it was by them and no one else. This is a kind of self-created immortality which is fascinating and incredible; a way that whatever happens, these crafters, these artisans will live on in the memories of those who indulge in their beautiful works.

I know weavers and engineers; archers and tree surgeons; Reiki masters and painters. Not all of these skills are about creating something to have and to hold, but they are all about honing a skill. This skill is honed to a point that, not only can you make a living from it, but by making your own living, you are bringing something positive to the world you live in.

The Celts are renowned for their impact on the history of art and crafts, and there are many beautiful examples of work from as far back as the Bronze Age, which all seem to have one thing in common – as well as the items and tools they made being practical, they are all beautiful as well. It seemed particularly important to the Celts that what they made not only showed an understanding of the tool, but displayed the artisan's skill by being ornate and beautiful, beyond what was required.

I mentioned witchcraft earlier and that term is ambiguous at best, but I use it to refer to a collection of skills that will ultimately be used to change the world around you in small ways to make it a more positive place. All the skills above, if used with this intent in mind, could be classed as a kind of witchcraft.

My own personal witchcraft includes the writing of poetry, song and music, and it *is* a magic; the power of a well played or well written song is undeniable. I have yet to meet anyone who is completely unaffected by music at some level, and that level is always emotional or psychological. I don't assume to be a master, indeed, I view myself as a novice because my focus changes too often; I have gone from being a keyboardist and songwriter in a very light hearted guitar band, to a front woman in a much heavier rock band, to playing folk and blues acoustically in a duo with a wonderful soul singer. While all these are still on the cards, I am in the process of recording some older songs in my own style, while also researching traditional folk music, with the help of others interested in the same types of songs. I've reworked a few of the folk songs into a more modern style, and have also recently created some devotional music and poetry for my ritual work.

My point is thus: music is a part of my life. Whatever I am doing, music surrounds me. If I am not creating, I am listening. This for me is a very deep connection to my Celtic heritage. There are so many examples of music in Celtic literature and writings influenced by it, and the music nearly always has magical connotations. I don't think my playing has the power to put armies to sleep (in fact I hope it doesn't!) but I do think that every time I sing a song that makes someone's hair stand on end, or makes them smile, or sniff back a tear, then I have achieved a little piece of magic that would make my Celtic ancestors proud. That is why no matter what else is going on in my life, I will always make time for music. That is my magic; melody is the voice I use to speak my spells.

Chapter Four

Taming the Wild –
Celts and their Creatures

Hey
Miss it once
Hey
Look up
Two jackdaws in a sycamore tree
One edged along the main branch
Blinking down at me in curiosity
Sharing the autumn sun
All three cloaked against the autumn wind
The two birds aren't hunting
Or foraging
Simply resting and being;
At the most, marking their territory:
Enjoying their existence
Reminding me not to feel guilty
About doing the same.

When I was a little girl my Dad found a crow. It had fallen from its nest and its parents wouldn't take it back. My Dad brought it home and we looked after it – which turned out to be a 'she' rather than an 'it'. We called her Megan, and she lived with us for months, happily hopping around the house and tormenting the cats. As she got towards adulthood, she became broody, and started to fly off, although returning later to roost with us, her surrogate corvids, in the living room. Eventually one day she didn't return, but from time to time for many years we saw her in the area – she was identifiable by missing feathers, scars of her accident as a fledgling.

When I was years older, not too long before I was ready to leave the nest myself, I found another crow; another baby. I was on the way back from my part-time job and walking across the grass behind the local reservoir overflow; a beauty spot (if you ignore the occasional dumped trolley!) and home to many varieties of wildlife. I spotted the crow from some distance away. He was very small but fully formed with the fluffiness of youth still upon him. Two adult crows were pecking at him and though he kept trying to fly away he couldn't manage it.

As I approached, the two adult crows flew away but the youngster was badly injured. He tried to hop along the grass but eventually stopped and lay shivering while I gently scooped him up. I carefully carried him home, walking slowly and smoothly so as not to jolt or jerk him. My parents were not massively surprised although they were taken aback by his injuries. We got a big shoe box and put some soft material in, and tried to feed him some ground up cat food. At first he wouldn't take it; then he ate a little, and then seemed to fluff up and go to sleep. I was worried the shock had all been too much and he would simply die, in the way birds can if they face too much trauma. I was exhausted myself and lay on the sofa to rest; within minutes I was asleep.

When I awoke, I felt an unfamiliar weight and warmth on my belly. I lifted my head and squinted sleepily: resting on my tummy, like a little ball of black fluff, was my rescue crow. He must have awoken and hopped up onto the sofa, deciding I was a much comfier option than his box! I was overwhelmed with a feeling of bonding with this tiny black creature, and he stayed with me for many years after this. At one point I moved into a house where I simply could not take him with me, so my Mum and Dad stepped in and said they would look after him. He's still living there now, 13 years later, happy and healthy. When he sees me he still fluffs himself up and clicks his beak at me, and takes little titbits from my fingers. I don't view him as a 'familiar' or similar. He is simply another creature who has honoured me by sharing his life with me.

Please note; despite my experience bonding with two crows it is *not recommended* that you try to take wild corvids home or wild animals of any kind – seek professional assistance. In both instances we had professional advice and my father was an experienced bird handler so we knew what we were doing.

The Celts understood that humans are not alone in this world as being *special*; they honoured *all* their creatures – cows, wolves, crows – and wove them into their stories and myths copiously. I take the time to ask my parents if they feel their love of animals is a hereditary thing, and if so, how it links back to the Celtic heritage in particular.

My Mum begins: 'I think that's one of the Celtic things that I really appreciate, the fondness for their animals and the way they use totemic creatures. I feel they had a deeper understanding of animals in some ways than people do now, or they appreciated them more as being creatures of another species; they didn't have the view that, 'This world is mine, these animals are mine; I can do what I want.' The Celts didn't have that.'

My Dad interjects: 'Apart from where cows were concerned.'

I point out that even though cattle were obviously used and often used hard, they were also respected and even revered as being of great value, and certainly owning a remarkable beast was a symbol of wealth and power. My Dad suggests that perhaps the cows and bulls were of totemic significance to the Irish Celts.

My Mum adds: 'They were more like Native Americans I would say in the way they behaved towards animals; you might eat the animals, you might even herd the animals, but you respect the animals, as being creatures of a different species, but not necessarily less than you.'

Dad: 'I think that attitude shows in this family as well, because, well look at us: there's a dog there, there's a cat somewhere within ten yards, there's Crowley [my beautiful rescue crow] and the rats! It's obviously within our gene structure somewhere.'

Mum: 'Like the people that used to live in the house with the pigs and everything in with them, all living together. It's like the dog [Megan, old black Labrador Alsatian cross, weary, slightly loose of bowel and slow of foot but loved and happy]; most people would say, 'I'd have had that dog put down a couple of years ago', but it's not something we'd even consider because she's happy in herself. The carpet's ruined and we have to clean up after her every day, but we just do it because...'

My sister interjects to point out that we wouldn't put a person down if they were in that state. I think that's the difference in the way we look at people and animals today: we see putting a dog down as a mercy because the animal is in pain, or suffering, or cannot look after itself anymore, yet the idea of euthanizing a human is abhorrent to most people, hence why it is illegal in so many places. I tend to find that the people I talk to who have closer relationships with both animals *and* humans understand that pain and suffering should be taken away *whatever* the species, and that they themselves would not want to live on in a vegetative state (for example), but that if they could be cared for and kept comfortable and happy, then they would expect to live, and they will give the same courtesy to the animals they bring into their lives.

My Mum adds: 'It's the same with Crowley; when we took him to the vet they said, 'You'll have to have him put down otherwise you'll have to look after him forever', and we said, 'What's wrong with that?''

I turn from the topic of how we look after animals and how they share our daily lives, either as companions or colleagues, to a point that interests me a great deal: animals are often used in the stories of the Celtic people to symbolise change, transformation, and are frequently used as symbols for a character in the story. They are also used to show that magic is afoot – for example a horse that is only half a horse,[30] or a red and white cow.[31] I query my parents: do they believe that in this reality, today, animals come into our lives at points of significance and points of change; are they symbols of magical things happening within our own lives?

Both: 'Yes, definitely.'

Dad says: 'I can point to an animal in question: Megan.'

My Mum joins in agreement: 'We'd just lost Amber [another big, beautiful dog who joined the family when my brother was a baby, whereas Megan came when my *sister* was a baby]; we'd gone to have her cremated, and that exact same day when we went and took her, there was a puppy and it was Megan. And Judith gave her to us! She didn't ask for any money or anything...'

Dad: '...Which is the remarkable part because she [Judith] doesn't do that. She's a professional breeder, but she just gave Megan to us.'

Mum: 'And she's [Megan is] 14 this year; by rights, going by what breed of dog she is, she should have lived to be about nine or ten. She's very special.'

I also point out that in the time they have lived at that house, there has probably been a crow present for more time than there has not, other than the short time Crowley lived with me in my own house. The Crow is a very strong Celtic symbol; you couldn't get much more on the nose!

My Mum laughs and agrees: 'That's true!'

I add: 'Not unless you had a wolf and a snake about the place as well!'

My Mum continues: 'And a cow!'

Dad points out: 'We did have a lurcher for a long time, who also just turned up when you think about it. That's the archetypal Irish dog.'

Mum: 'You know the skinny dog, greyhound shape.'

Dad: 'If you look at the knot work, that's the dog that you see in the knot work. It was of stupendous importance to the Celtic people.'

Mum: 'Horses as well. Not that we've got those!'

According to the Coligny Calendar, one of the months of the Celts (at least on the continent) was called the month of horses, indicating some cultural significance, whether through herding, riding or using the beast for meat and milk. Horses have been a part of western culture for probably about 5,000 years, and maybe for even longer in the east.

My Mum thinks back to my family's involvement with horses: 'I think that's one thing when Kirsten went to learn to ride; we could take her because we had the money at the time and we thought, 'That's a good thing because everybody should learn to ride', which seems pointless and futile in our society, but to me that was like, 'Yeah, that's what you do'.'

My Dad agrees: 'That's the way I feel as well; I learnt to ride as young as I could.'

I should point out here that although this love of horses may be genetic, and indeed I adore the big eyed beasts, the natural affinity for riding them has not passed down to me. The one and only time I rode a horse, a great, stroppy black beast, I hung on for dear life and could not be coaxed even to sit up properly for fear of tumbling to a muddy death! Having said that, I would love to learn properly, but I think it would be much like learning to drive has been: a slow and arduous process for me.

In Appendix B at the end of the main book I have included some notes on the significance of particular animals within Celtic culture, according to the literature we have to support this. One of the most interesting points I come across again and again is how the links between human and animal seem to almost blur. Characters within the story are forever transforming themselves into animals; hounds, pigs, wolves, eels, cows and various birds all figure in various different versions of numerous tales. In nearly all of these, there is either a fight or a chase, so the transformation implies that in these confrontations *being human isn't enough.*

I think this, more than anything, indicates the reverence the Celts had for these creatures. They either thought that the animal was better in some way to deal with the situation: the pig could root around unnoticed; the hound was swift; the bird could fly away. Or alternatively, they were so fond of metaphor that the transformation was actually a dramatic description of a human characteristic so beyond what was to be expected, that one could only believe they had become an animal.

Perhaps the Morrigan was so fierce in her battle rush that she merely seemed as unstoppable as a heifer at the head of a stampede. Perhaps the poetic nature of the original storyteller wouldn't allow them to pass up an opportunity to embellish the battle according to their audience. (Remember that all these tales would have been passed orally before being recorded by scholars many centuries later.)

This again shows that the audience in question must have had a great respect for the creatures concerned, otherwise there would have been nothing to compel the original tale weaver to include these dramatic devices. That's presuming, indeed, that dramatic devices is what they were. I can heartily recommend reading Táin Bó Cúailnge for a good example of animals with 'primary' roles in a story. The main gist of the tale is the importance of two particular bulls, although that's only the tip of the iceberg really.

All my friends who follow some link to their Celtic heritage have had profound experiences with animals at some point in their lives. We've already talked about my parents' experiences with their 'hounds', Amber and Megan, appearing when they were most needed. Many of my friends own cats and treat them exactly as if they are a part of the family, as do I. I don't think we see them as 'familiars' in the story book witch sense, but we do see them as companions. They are not 'simply animals', they are a vital part of our lives, and remind us to respect the other creatures that live all around us, within our homes and without.

Chapter Five

Inspiration from the Elf Mounds

So what words whisper from the elf mounds; what wind breathes from beneath the hollow hills where fairies dwell and myths were born? In other words, how many of us today still feel inspired by the tales of ancient Celtic warriors and wise folk? Which parts of our lives do these stories creep into the most? What do our ancestors still truly have a hand in? What is the *meat* of modern Celtic influence? Well a quick 'Google' search on the word 'Celt' will find you brewing techniques that are based on Celtic history; BBC Wales has a site dedicated to the history of the Iron Age Celts and the word CELT is used as an acronym by organisations in fields ranging from teaching to audio compression!

Let's take a look at the images section now: maps of the Celtic migration across Europe; knot work; helmets; warriors fighting in great battles; beards, shields and swords; jewellery, sandals and musical instruments. Take a look around when you're out and about and see how many tattoos you see that incorporate Celtic knot work, and how many sterling silver Celtic crosses you can see in the windows of jewellers.

When the paths were resurfaced outside a new housing estate near where I live, there were some elder trees, ancient and gnarled, that were untouched even though they were growing right out of the pavement that otherwise was completely dug out and overhauled. If the trees were left untouched for superstitious reasons (oh how I wish I could talk to the people who did that stretch of road!) those superstitions almost certainly stem from the Celtic reverence for certain trees. This seems to be carried into the names of local establishments. Without travelling more than a couple of miles in any direction, I can visit Copper Beech

Nursery; Hollybush Children's Centre; Holly Bush Farm Conservation Centre; Beech Medical Centre. My own doctor is housed within the Hawthorn Medical Centre!

These names show the importance we still place upon trees, which almost certainly stems from our Celtic ancestors. The druidic reverence for certain trees led Robert Graves to create the Celtic Tree Calendar which, somewhat unfortunately, has become used as an actual 'Celtic Calendar' for some people. It has, as far as I can understand, no real basis in Celtic timekeeping or astrology, but it does, again, show how deeply we are influenced by accounts of Celtic society and how much we want to recreate aspects of that in our modern lives.

Sir Terry Pratchett, an incredibly popular British author, created the 'Lords and Ladies', elves that while being beautiful are fierce, ruthless and inhuman. There are similarities here of course to the Fae, who are often described as incredibly beautiful and powerful, yet they too are not quite human. They also can possess great cruelty, as in the story of the death of Cían, Lugh's father, who is stoned to death in hatred by a rival family until all that is left is a 'poor miserable, broken heap'.[32] Terry also created the Nac Mac Feegle, who actually live inside the burial mounds of kings, harking back to the tales that the fairies will take you under the hollow hills to their home. In these tales, often the protagonist finds what they believe is their heart's desire but returns a hundred years later, to find everyone they love is dead and gone. In one of Terry Pratchett's stories, this would probably be because the Nac Mac Feegle had drunk them under a tiny table!

Terry himself implies in his introduction to The Folklore of Discworld that tales and superstitions should not be forgotten as they are part of the history of who we are and how we got here. Any homage to these ancient tales is a great example of the way Celtic culture still inspires modern artists and writers. Through their modern art, they will inspire others to go seek out these ancient tales for themselves. We see the same stories being used over and over in a thousand different ways, keeping them alive to pass down to our children and future descendants.

Currently on television we have True Blood which is based on Charlaine Harris' very popular Southern Vampire Mysteries. There are a variety of supernatural creatures here but the fairies are very interesting: human in appearance yet inhuman within; old, powerful and able to change their appearance; they also have (in the books) very Gaelic sounding names which hark back again to the tales of the Tuatha Dé Danann.

I asked Charlaine if she had intentionally based her fairy creations on the Celtic myths and legends and she agreed she had, but very loosely. The evidence of this is shown in some of the names she chooses for the fairy characters: Niall Brigant, Breandan and Neave, for example. Breandan is Gaelic for Prince; Niall means Champion and Brigant is possibly derived from the Celtic goddess Brigantia and generally means high, lofty, elevated or divine. Neave is an anglicised version of Niamh, which is Gaelic for 'Radiant'. Again, these are tiny droplets of Celtic culture seeping into something that is modern, vibrant, and extremely popular.

When I was very young I had only heard a few tales of the Tuatha Dé Danann – the tales of Tir-na-Nog from my father, and a few others from books. The catalyst for my inspiration to seek more knowledge was a very modern creation; a band called Horslips and their album The Táin, of course based on Táin Bó Cúailnge, the Cattle Raid. Not only was the music fascinating – a mix of traditional folk and rock – but the stories held within the words absolutely mesmerized me.

After listening to The Táin over and over, I got my hands on another of their albums, The Book of Invasions, a name you will recognise already if you've been reading the chapters of this book in order! The album is split into three sections, based on the idea of a Celtic symphony: Geantrai, Goltrai and Suantrai, which mean joyful, sorrowful and lullaby. Horslips themselves describe the three as the three principal categories of old Irish song; the joyful strain, the lamenting strain and the sleep strain. I spent hours with my mandolin and flageolet copying and playing these songs, and imagining the scenes of the stories as the music wound its way around me. The incredible depth of the love stories:

> *Let me ask you this one question*
> *Is it really such a sin?*
> *To love too much, to be closer than touch when there was no way we could win...* [33]

The violence of Cú Chulainn's conquests:

> *Two heads are better than none*
> *A hundred heads are so much better than one!* [34]

And the betrayal of kings and queens and lovers:

> *You can fool them all right; but can you fool the beast?* [35]

Horslips are a prime example of how these fantastic stories of an amazing people have inspired a new and marvellously unique retelling of these tales. The band's use of traditional tunes and songs keep another aspect of Irish culture alive and thriving, making this mythology accessible to those not only interested in tales and legends, but also in music and revelry. The commercial success of Horslips in the 1970s meant a whole new generation was introduced to the tales of the Tuatha Dé Danann, and received a unique glimpse into this ancient and, to most people, almost alien culture. Horslips have complemented their music with a website detailing the stories of their albums and the history of some of the traditional music incorporated into the songs. For anyone unfamiliar with the Celtic legends, these albums are a comprehensive and very entertaining introduction. The band recently reformed after 24 years, and are still incredibly popular, showing how interest in Irish culture in particular and Celtic culture in general have not waned during the decades since they originally disbanded.

In the appendices and glossary you will find, next to some of the terminology, examples of how the word or phrase has been used in popular culture, and some of the uses are quite surprising. There are many examples from modern literature, from authors who have been inspired by local folklore or their own heritage. But you may be surprised to find that the modern video game industry has not escaped the influence of Celtic legend. I love this; it shows how deep the story goes, and is a great indicator of exactly how long it has the potential to live for.

Chapter Six

Speaking with the Ancestors

Home is where heartache fades and headaches ease. Home is where colour seeps in and stains grey. Home is where the volume is switched as loud as you want, which can simply mean silence. Home is where a hole inside of you is filled once you arrive. Home is where voices you only hear once a year fill you with joy, or voices you hear every day still make you tingle with anticipation. Home is where food and warmth are pressed upon you with no desire for reciprocation. Home is care and comfort. Home is falling in love. Home is sometimes falling out. But home is always the smells that evoke the strongest memories; the stillness of a breath or the wind upon a face in the open; home is great stones in walls or circles; home is where you take it, and where you make it. I am home, and I am going home.

The truth is that everyone was formed by their ancestors in some way. If you deny any connection to your ancestors, then that is a conscious decision which, in itself, partially shapes who you are. Even by denying them, which is absolutely your right to do, and you may have extraordinarily good reasons for doing so, you have changed yourself in some way by making that decision. I have accepted this, and instead of being ignorant of the people who essentially made me, I have decided to try to find a connection to them via the myths and legends that they spawned; the tales they told and the beings they revered are part of their culture, and now they are part of mine. I heartily recommend to anyone to seek out something of what made you who you are today; perhaps something you have little knowledge of, or something you could feel closer to, and try to forge a bond; try to find a point where that means something to you as a modern individual; as a vibrant and unique human being. I discovered the Tuatha Dé Danann. Who knows what you may find?

Very few of us begin this life completely alone. Few of us would survive if we did, and those who maybe do begin alone and manage to survive, are usually taken in and cared for by someone later in life, meaning that not a single one of us is the sum entirely of their own being; every individual is inspired and altered by at least one other living being.

Think about the people in your life who have inspired you in some way; these don't have to be your elders; they may be your peers, your children, your neighbours or their relatives. Look at how they behave in relation to their parents or grandparents. See the similarities? The differences? These are things that are often hard to see in ourselves, but much easier to see in others. The way one woman might avoid drinking because she sees the effect it had on a parent. The way one man joins a specific club because his parents did and he's keeping that tradition alive. Parents asking for childcare advice from *their* parents, and conversely learning from the perceived mistakes of their parents, to better themselves; to evolve, one generation at a time.

My friend Chris talks about using the tales and history of our ancestors much in the same way – as a huge library of information and experience that we can dip into as and when we need to, in order to help us out with the decisions we have to make daily. As well as this, we also have the help of our ancestors; we may learn from our parents and grandparents, some of us even further back than that. But sometimes we forget that what we are learning from them, they learned, in some part, from their parents and grandparents and this goes right back to the beginning of humanity. There is a part of every one of us that is in some tiny way influenced by a human being, or human beings, so ancient and removed from our species as it is *now* as to be unrecognisable as what *we* would refer to as a person. There are also lots more tiny parts of you made from the wisdom and insight and indeed the physical genetics of every single descendant of that proto-human.

This to me is incredible; just thinking that the simple fact that we are alive means we are connected to the very beginning of our race, and that we are the living memory and history of a whole species. I contain within me the sum of everyone who has gone before me, and although I no doubt share that with thousands of others who may, in some small part, share my ancestry, I am a unique creation of a particular concoction of genetics, experience and chance.

My first port of call on this journey into my Celtic ancestry is with my parents. They are the ones who introduced me to the stories of the Celts and the scholars who wrote about them, and also to the idea that magic is alive in the world. So what made them choose this aspect of their ancestry to focus on when naming me and my siblings? Do they see themselves as the living progeny of the Celts or are they simply enamoured of the ideas spawned by the fantasy and myth surrounding them? Have they ever tried to connect more deeply to their own ancestors, in the same way I am doing now?

My Dad begins our discussion by debating the existence of the Celts at all, which at first makes me panic; please don't tell me I've had the wrong end of the stick all these years! But he goes on to explain all the conflicting information on the people we call Celts, and the fact that we tend to group together tribes that may never have had any connection at all, and call them all Celts, despite the fact that they most probably never called themselves that at all. He says this is one of the reasons he's always had such a deep interest in them.

'It is our heritage, but it is confusing!' he adds.

My Mum agrees with this, saying: 'It's an interesting part of history that no one knows all that much about, it's just hints and things, and I think from the point of view of writing you can make up anything because there's very little actual 'fact' to go on. There is a lot of mythology, but how much of that is based on fact and how much is exaggeration; like the Bible, you know, there's things in there that couldn't possibly be; people tend to (when they're doing mythology) make everything larger than life.'

My Dad follows this up with: 'One of the things that I find fascinating about this era, is not only is there a strong oral tradition which has been handed down, sometimes obviously badly, because it doesn't always make apparent sense; you've got to think at some point it must have made sense, otherwise it wouldn't have passed down. But as well as that there's a really strong body of archaeological evidence, sadly bugger all in the way of written, which is understandable since not many people were writing a lot at that time anyway. Even in Mediterranean culture writing was pretty unusual. It's only when you get into the Middle East that writing becomes more common, and even then the chances of it being written on something portable are fairly slim; well the chances of it being written on something weighing a few tons are a lot more likely.'

My Mum adds: 'I think what interests me about the Celts is that they were kind of like proto-Vikings; they were like the Normans who later sort of spread everywhere, and they were kind of like Norse people, they'd come from there and gone to France and everywhere. The Celts just sort of set off and went all over the place. Even as far as Macedonia and places like that.'

One of the aspects that interests me about the Celtic migration is that as these tribes or communities moved, especially in the east to west migration, they seemed to have absorbed bits and bats of the various cultures they had contact with. By the time they were established in Ireland, these aspects would have found their way into the tales and stories of the land and the people there, so it's no wonder, to me, that we see similarities to Greek and even Egyptian myths in many of the Celtic tales that are still alive today.

For example, the triple nature of the Morrigan and her association with death and rebirth is akin to Hekate, who was widely revered in the Mediterranean, particularly Greece, during the periods that the Celts may have been travelling through these parts. This is not to say that Hekate and the Morrigan are one and the same, but it possibly explains the similarities in how they were portrayed. I ask my Dad if he thinks the east to west migration is responsible for bleeding from one culture into the other.

My Dad ponders this then answers: 'Well no, you've got to look at it along the other direction as well because we're always concentrating on the east to west, but if you actually have a look at the migratory patterns, you'll find that there's quite a lot going west to east. They weren't, as many people imagine, expanding in one direction; they seem to have complete and utter randomness about where they were off. You know the stories behind the colonisation of Ireland? You know there's more than one wave?'

Of course there is a pause for a good eye roll and sigh here as I confirm to my father that yes, I still remember the Book of Invasions.

'Well if you follow that you'll see that there's an outgoing wave at one point, who return later, but they take, well I'm not sure how many years. But if you look in the Middle East about the same sort of time span, you'll find that there's a sudden influx of people from, well, nobody knows where, and archaeologically there's an awful lot of similarities between them and what I would describe as proto Celts. Anthropologically and archaeologically the people we're talking about as being Celts *aren't* and they *weren't* [Celts], because they're [from] long before. If you pin the Celts down as Bronze and Iron age, mainly Iron, well the first set of movements happens long before then.'

I explain that this is why I'm trying to stay away from the history in this book, because as my Dad says, it's so debatable.

And as my Mum described earlier, the myths and legends tell us something of the people and how they liked to tell tales, but which of these tales is an exaggeration of a real event, and which are complete fantasy? We debate this briefly and I go on to ask what made my parents want to absorb some of the aspects of Celtic culture into their own lives, for example the paths that they've followed spiritually, and the annual festivals they celebrate.

Dad volunteers: 'Being a Yorkshire person, for me, it's [the connection to his heritage] always been there. This area is, it was rather, the Parisii and Brigantes; depends which part of Leeds you stand in as to which one of the two groups it is. I don't even know to be honest, because of the lack of written records, how the two got on with each other.

'So for all I know they might have been best buds! But for me that's, ever since I can remember, I've had a fascination – don't ask me how or where it came from! I don't know, because my parents certainly weren't involved.'

I remember that my Nana and Granddad on my Dad's side were a bit baffled by Dad's forays into the exploration of his Celtic ancestry, but having said that they were involved in some ancestor hunting of their own. They were involved with The Sealed Knot, an English Civil War re-enactment group, and applied themselves with gusto to the roles of their forebears. So this love of history was obviously passed down. I look to my Mum to see where her links to her Celtic heritage began.

'When I was little everybody was Irish and that was kind of the thing, you know, 'Your Irish heritage', but it was a lot more modern than that because people would think about things like the Troubles and being Catholic and being nationalistic about Ireland. I don't remember anybody ever really going into anything about the Celts. I didn't really find out about them 'til later on. [It was] Dad [who] told me [about them].

There is a look of disbelief from Father here!

Mum continues: 'Really! Because before that I was really more interested in the ancient world, the Greeks and Arthurian legends. To be honest although I accept the Celts as part of my heritage, I don't think I'm really all that into them. I am interested in them from a historical point of view, but as far as their myths and legends go; I don't really feel Wicca is necessarily Celtic. [Resounding agreement from around the room at this point]. I think of it as being more British.

'I'd really like to know more about the Picts, I have this fascination with Brownies. I'm really interested in knowing whether the Brownies or the stories about them were actually based on small people who lived here before the Celts came.'

My Dad points out that there is a great deal of controversy about whether the Picts really existed, but Mum continues: 'I think I tend to be more interested in the mythological history of Britain as a whole rather than the Tuatha Dé Danann as such, whom I see as more of a probably historical bunch of people.'

I'm interested in this view point as it goes back to what I was saying earlier, that my main fascination is that the Tuatha Dé Danann are a people, rather than a race of deities, or at least the stories may be based on real people, rather than myths in their entirety. I'm also fascinated and surprised that my Mum claims to not have that keen an interest in the Celtic aspects of British heritage. I point out that my parents must have been pretty keen on Celtic mythology at some point, because look at my name, and my brother is Conal and my sister is Kirsten Róisín. Also, my Dad's old business, making miniatures, was called Tír na nÓg. I remind them of all the tales of the Tuatha Dé Danann they told me as a child. Has that fascination ebbed off over the years, and where did it initially come from?

My Dad decides ultimately his interest has never waned: 'I don't know where it came from, as I say I personally have no obvious Irish ancestry, well I do but not within living memory. Mum's is more obvious.'

Mum agrees: 'Mine is more current. Most of my ancestors were Irish, one way or another, originally Irish or perhaps Scots because they went back and forth a lot, or the sort of Anglo Irish which is like the Talbots and so forth. I think those stories are very accessible aren't they, because there's a lot of others similar; you get a lot of Welsh Celtic stories like the Mabinogion and so forth; a lot of the [mythology of the] rest of Britain is missing, so you tend to go for what you've got, in the sense of these are old stories from past times.'

Dad adds: 'I think you might have put your finger on the spot where [the interest in Celtic culture] came from with me then, because I've always been somebody who doesn't like there to be an unaccounted-for vacuum. That's probably what prompted me to look, but so long ago I can't remember exactly.'

My Mum likens the apparent gaps in British ancient history and mythology to folk music: 'I mean when I was little my Dad used to be like: 'Here's this Irish folk music'. Like the Dubliners, dear me, and I was told: 'There is no English folk music, there isn't any. It doesn't exist'. When I started going to folk clubs and stuff and I got into Steeleye Span and all that kind of thing I was like, 'But there's just masses of it!''

My Dad postulates: 'For me it was probably the lack of, or the anonymity of, the English identity. Because that's what it is, isn't it, we're anonymous.'

I don't entirely agree with my father here; I don't think there is a lack of English identity altogether, but I agree that it is fractured, which makes sense really because for most of our history our little island has been a mass of warring tribes. Religions and traditions have been absorbed and reabsorbed and even something as common and ritual (as in repeated year after year) as Christmas is an amalgamation of so many symbols and religions it's hard to know where to begin! We have Christmas trees for bringing greenery into the house, fires for encouraging the sun to return, Yule logs; well I don't want to teach you to suck eggs, but it's a fantastic example of how England, and Britain generally, is a massive melting pot of cultures, something I personally find fascinating and pleasing.

However, I can accept that because there remains no *definitive* English tradition to follow, to follow those of your Irish Celtic ancestors would have a great attraction, especially because they have such a strong and long lived mythological cycle. I ask my parents what it is specifically about Irish Celtic tales, such as Táin Bó Cúailnge, that resonates with them. Why are these stories still so accessible today?

My Mum begins: 'You can see the stereotypical Irish mentality starting off there can't you, what's mine is mine and what's yours is mine as well. There's a lot of fighting going on and a lot of drinking and stuff. It's all got that kind of cheerfulness to it.'

The Tuatha Dé Danann, although revered as deities and supernatural beings, are very flawed and therefore very human. I ask my Dad if he thinks this is part of what makes them so appealing.

He replies: 'Definitely. It makes them more accessible.'

My Mum expands on this: 'Because people, pantheistic people, tend to make their gods in the image of themselves, don't they. Like the Greek pantheon, and the Roman (which were really the Greek ones which they borrowed) and the Celts too; they didn't try to make their gods any better than they were themselves really. They reflected the people rather than trying to set them apart and make them into something unattainable. Because, take Christianity; they've taken what may or may not have been a real person and tried to make him into something that nobody could ever be.

'It's a bit like when you see super models and there's a lot of people try and look like that, but it's impossible because either they don't have the bone structure or just nobody could ever look like that... What I'm saying is the Christian god and probably the

Jewish god and the Muslim religion; they all encourage a person to aspire to be something that is actually going to totally stress them out, because it's against nature.

'Celtic deities – they don't expect too much of you, in fact they don't really expect anything of you. They're kind of like great big people. I think that's the appeal of them, that they are very much like people, only on a larger scale.'

Dad adds: 'There's no hard and fast, good or bad either. That's one of the things I really love about them.'

Mum ponders the difference between the ethical stances: 'Yeah, well, there's a whole different kind of moral philosophy there isn't there? If I can steal it then it's mine, and if you can take it back well it's yours again, fair enough.'

This seems to me to be more about strength than morality as we understand it today. In all the confrontations in Celtic tales it is the stronger person who generally wins, but they may be stronger of wit, or of magic, rather than just strong of arm. Glory was given to the greater person, and rarely was anyone told, 'Hey, that's just not right!'

My Mum agrees and adds that it's probably not good for people in general to tell them too many things are 'wrong' or 'bad'; that's how people end up with ridiculous hang ups, and also the inability to deal with ethical and moral debate on their own merit.

My parents had the opportunity to live and work in Ireland for a time, near Dublin. I wonder, particularly of my Mum with her direct links to Irish ancestry, if being in Ireland made them feel closer, more connected to their heritage somehow? They both agree that in some ways they did, but that they also feel that connection in Yorkshire, where we live, because of the fact this is where more recent ancestors chose to settle.

My Dad adds to this: 'Make of this what you will, but there are three places I've ever felt at home: here, Ireland and Cyprus. So what the heck that tells you I don't know!'

My Mum chips in: 'The Normans went to Cyprus...'

Dad grins. 'I was about to say you might mention the famous words Normans or Crusaders...'

My Dad's ancestry leans more towards the Norman conquests so again, it's likely his ancestors on this side had been across the Mediterranean and surrounding areas. I point out again that it's just as likely that his Celtic ancestors had trekked across Cyprus and related place. We go on to discuss some of the artefacts found across Europe that indicate this meshing of cultures, and we get onto the highly decorative nature of some of the work attributed to the Celts. I wonder if this is something else we have inherited, the apparent love of physically pleasing objects?

My Mum is adamant this is the case: 'When you make something or you get something, I have the idea that it shouldn't be just plain, that it should be something that looks nice as well as being useful, and those two things go together to me. It's not just something pretty and not just something useful but the two things together.'

I completely understand this desire; even as a tiny child playing in the garden, building little houses of sticks and stones, I would decorate everything, even if it was only a plant pot. I would dig up chalk to draw spirals and circles on stones or pots, and weave stars out of grass and hang them around the dens I made. It wasn't enough to have something practical; it had to be a thing of beauty too. Even if that was the childlike beauty of handmade toys and basic art. But just like my Mum says, it's rare to have something beautiful if it's not also useful for something. I love making candles, of all colours and scents, but although they are pretty and smell good, they tend to be tailored for the person I am making them for – a scent to promote sleep, or to calm; a colour to match a particular room or brighten the mood and of course a candle is, at its essence, a practical item. I think all of us in my family create things like this in some way – useful items, but always carefully made to bring beauty into our lives.

I wonder, as some of this book is about the *magic* of the Celts and of modern day practitioners, if my parents have had any experience of actually *meeting* their ancestors? Have they felt their presence in their day-to-day lives? Have they had a face-to-face confrontation with one of the Tuatha Dé Danann? There is a little more detail on this in a later chapter, Fingers through the Veil, but my Mum begins by saying she has never seen a spirit, and that she has seen a ghost. Confused, I ask her what the difference is.

My Mum explains: 'Well a ghost is what's left of something that lived here and a spirit might have been here, but you don't *know* do you, it's from a different plane I would say: it didn't originate here. Probably!'

My Dad is thoughtful: 'I like your way of looking at it. Personally though, I wouldn't put the two apart; I'd say they're akin. But I don't know how close akin they are so I'm just going to leave it at that and say OK, it's a ghost, or a demonic presence.'

My Mum conjectures: 'I think we just call things spirits when they're perhaps ghosts from so long ago we don't know when it was.'

Dad adds: 'Or *what* it was, sometimes.'

Mum: 'And then there are things like elementals.'

My parents had mentioned a trip to Rudston Monolith where they had experienced some cold, tingling sensations. I wonder if this is the indication that they are in the presence of something unseen; something otherworldly. My Mum talks about the sensation of seeing sparkles that are traditionally a sign that you are on the verge of some world *beyond* this world. The sparkling at the corner of one's vision; the glint of tiny lights that simply should not be there; we all agree that although none of us know what this experience really *means,* we all maintain an open mind about such things.

My Dad adds: 'I think that one way of looking at that is it's a way of telling ourselves that we could, at this point, enter another state of consciousness, a bit like, sorry to bring this down to earth so much, but a bit like somebody going on an acid trip. Physically [the person on acid is] still here, but their mind is, pardon the pun, off with the faeries. Might not be the right kind of faeries though!'

My Mum isn't sure about this, as being under the effect of hallucinogens is *not* the same as experiencing something that is actually there, just slightly beyond our normal range of experience.

Dad explains: 'I meant they're changing the state of their consciousness in some way and I think, well, the Celts knew this: you can change your state of consciousness through lots of other things like music, dance; a whole gamut of experiences, sensory and abstract. I may be wrong here but maybe the sparkling or feeling of cold or whatever happens is a way of trying to alert you to the possibility that this would be a good place to make the change.'

Mum agrees and adds: 'I think you become aware of more things than you normally are aware of, but what those things are; that's debateable isn't it.'

Dad continues: 'To me, even if it's just a way of getting in touch with part of your inner self, that's important. It's a useful activity. That makes it sound so mundane. It's like an alarm bell in a way. Like something's trying to say 'Wake up! There's a dream around the corner. ''

I postulate that perhaps these feelings or sights are a form of trigger, a way of saying right, now you have an opportunity to experience something marvellous. Ultimately, it is up to you to do something about it.

Dad agrees, and Mum adds: 'I think at moments like that, you tend to become aware of the past or perhaps of the connection with the past. It's almost like you're standing at a railway station [linked to] the past, the future and the present; you're standing at *present* railway station, but the time is going by you and when these things [the sparkles or tingling] happen and you find a place where the actual railway station is, you can become aware of the whole train; all the carriages – you can sense that continuity. It is almost like entering a different state of consciousness where you're aware not just in space but in time as well.'

I love this analogy, that we are travelling on a train of time, on our own carriage that is always moving on and although it moves from past to future, it is always and forever simply in the present. Normally we'll sit happily in our own carriage, watching our own life go on down the tracks. But occasionally, we may trigger something that suddenly makes us aware of the other carriages, and the passengers therein; the people further back in our own carriage – our mothers and fathers, our grandparents and perhaps our great grandparents. Yet through the little walkway into the carriage behind, there are more people, still travelling onwards, still part of our train but normally just out of sight, only manifest in the genetic traits we share with the rest of the people on our carriage. Not just eye colour and hair colour, but the skills and abilities we nurture too.

We can see where it all came from: the great singing voice, or the perfect throwing arm; the instinctive gardener, or the brilliant mathematician. This eye opening, this new awareness, allows us to go and stand at the buffet with the people who came before us, lets us move down the train of history a little and feel the connection to the past, and the people who lived there. I wonder if it's also possible that when we feel weird and disoriented in places of great history, perhaps we are connecting slightly to the future as well, to the potential energy of those who will come after us: squinting through the glass to the carriages beyond our own.

So we've talked about experiences with those who have come before us, and those who may come after us. Now what about the mythical figures from Celtic mythology? Do any of them have any particular resonance for my parents? Instantly my Dad says his is obviously the Dagda, and my Mum states that she likes Brigid. I politely correct my mother's English pronunciation of the name and she replies that she is not even going to attempt the Gaelic pronunciation! Even my attempt kind of sounds like someone clearing their throat noisily, so I don't begrudge her the Anglicisation.

We get into a bit of discussion about the many different pronunciations and variants of her name. '*Breed*' is mentioned as a very common one, along with Brigit, Bride and Bridie. My Mum says that Bridie is still a common Irish name and that she used to work with someone called Bridie. We all turn out to have worked with or known someone called Bridie who worked in a caring profession of some sort, and we ponder the 'coincidence' of this: named after a caring, nurturing mother goddess, and drawn towards caring, nurturing professions. Not necessarily the influence of their forebears, but certainly a pleasant serendipity. I turn to my Dad now: what is it about the Dagda that stands out for him?

He replies: 'I don't know to be honest, I almost imagine him as a sort of Celtic Brian Blessed type character: a character and a cauldron that are both spewing forth all the time.'

My Mum adds: 'I like the Leanen Sídhe, which isn't actually a god. When she takes a fancy to poets and musicians she takes them away and teaches them how to be better at it. But they don't live very long.'

'That's the price,' notes my Dad.

Mum confirms: 'There's always a price.'

Dad continues: 'The Leanen Sídhe is looked upon as sort of a Celtic vampire; that's probably the best way to describe it.'

Mum points out: 'But she does actually give you something for it.'

Dad: 'There's usually an exchange somewhere in any of the Celtic stories.'

Moving away from the ancient tales to the more modern

versions of Pagan religion that my parents have been involved in, I wonder if they think their genetic and subconscious connection to their Celtic heritage moved them towards the Wiccan path that they ended up on.

My Dad agrees with this assumption: 'Definitely. I would say it had a lot to do with it. I started out looking more towards what I'd describe as hermetic thoughts, things like the Qabbalah. All the time, [there was] something deep within, and I'd be looking at something at a genetic level: I'm fairly convinced by what I know of our biological structure [I should point out here that my Dad is a successful bio-chemist] that memory is not just confined to up here [the brain]. Our whole body seems to be storing some of it.

'This is an odd story; I may have told you some of it before, I don't know whether I have or not. My Mum, your Gran, when she was asleep she could speak relatively fluent Spanish. When she was awake she couldn't, but asleep, she would sleep talk, and sometimes you could make out sentences and it was definitely relatively fluent Spanish. Where that came from – I'm blowed if I know. She'd no idea because she's never been to Spain. Being brought up in Ipswich I wouldn't imagine she knew many Spanish people either. To me that's proof positive. It's like other skills that as individuals we seem to have built in. From an early age I was always a very good shot [with a firearm]. That's not something, as a youngster, you practise. So obviously there is something about memory that goes back, so all I can assume is that at some point I managed to get in touch with a part of my ancestry that's suddenly thought, 'Right, I'm coming through to this century!'

Interested that genetic memory can steer us, I wonder if my parents came to the Wiccan path separately.

They both confirm this is so and my Mum tells me a bit about how she found her way there: 'My Dad was interested in it; I don't know why really because he didn't seem like that kind of person. We had one of Gardner's books on witchcraft; I read that so I knew something about it. I knew somebody who had a weird room in their house that felt very peculiar, and it turned out they were interested in magic, so I got to know more about it from that, then I found the Sorcerer's Apprentice, which was a shop in Leeds. I just sort of went on from there. I wasn't really interested in being a Wiccan as such; I was more interested in what you might call ceremonial magic. When I met Dad I got into Wicca.'

My Dad ponders that there are certainly elements of ceremonial magic within Wicca, and my Mum goes on to talk about her magical path.

'Yeah, I think as time's gone on it's become more important to me. It's made more sense. I like the sense that you're doing something that bears some relation to what people have been doing all along. We don't really need fire festivals now, but then again looking out of the window perhaps we do!'

I should pause here to explain that at this point during the English Summer we have had record amounts of rainfall and the deluge shows no signs of slowing right now. Everything is sodden and the cloud seems endless; a bit depressing even for the hardiest 'all weather' fan. Everyone I know is just hoping for that one sunny day to dry out and get out of the house!

Still thinking about fire festivals to drive back the rain Mum sighs. 'Maybe we need a good few more of them.'

This is exactly what I'm trying to get at: if anything, what is the relevance in our modern world of having a great fire, trying to draw back the sun, and all the other rituals based on and around the seasons?

My Mum thinks about this: 'I think it keeps you grounded. We live on the Earth; the Earth is important – it's our home. People have now come to realise that it's important that we look after the planet and the eco-systems therein. Basically, I think Pagans have known that all along any way. That's what the festivals and ceremonies really mean: that we're all a part of the same ball of mud spinning around the sun.'

I wonder if that's true; that there is a line of people going back, in our ancestry, that have always had the best interests of the land they live in at heart. Did our ancestors look after the environment they lived in even before people started waving the 'Green Flag' for re-using and recycling?

My Mum says: 'Well not recycling so much because I think there's only been a brief period where people didn't do that; when clothes suddenly became remarkably cheap.'

It does seem that we've gone through a strange journey as consumers over the past century: from not being able to afford to throw anything away, to suddenly being thrilled at being able to afford new things all the time, to finally realising that there's another reason why we should hang onto things and not throw everything away: because we're destroying the planet. There has only been a brief period of utter consumerism but it has been massively destructive.

Dad points out: 'Here in Britain, talk to any elderly people, and you'll find that they talk about things which make you go, hang on, that's like recycling. It was just called by different names. I'd say it was the generation who were born probably mid 60s onwards up to the mid-70s who were the worst culprits of the consumer generation.'

I point out that their children and their children's children carry it on; it seems they think either the state of the world doesn't affect them, or they *can't* affect it; like nothing they do would have an impact so why bother.

My Dad agrees: 'It's like they have no self-esteem or self-worth because they've been pushed under the thumb, as it were.'

Mum adds: 'And the educational system has failed everybody. And the governments. Leaving that aside, when I say grounded, I mean literally: thinking of the Earth, being a part of the Earth. You have to think about the seasons and you have to think about agriculture as well. For a long time it seemed very irrelevant to everybody but now that people are short of money people are growing their own [food] and people are worried about pesticides and so on. People are going back to appreciating how things work, how things come out of the soil and the cycle of one thing feeding upon another.'

Dad is nodding: 'I'm in full agreement with that. There are a few scientific things I could add. Have you ever noticed what it's like the day after bonfire night?'

My Dad and I had this discussion many times when I was a child. If bonfire night is dry enough to be a success, with many bonfires, then the next day is always fine. Smoky, hazy but dry and fair. The sheer volume of fires literally sends any clouds packing.

Dad carries on: 'That's a good scientific reason why these festivals can seem to improve the environment, because they actually do improve the environment, briefly!'

Surely pumping loads of wood smoke out into the atmosphere can't be great? Or would it not have had so much impact when our population was smaller?

My Dad believes the opposite: 'You'd be surprised at the amount of impact it can have. You've got to think, this is what's happening on a daily basis, normally [cooking fires etc.] and yet this one day of the year, we're going to multiply that a dozen fold, or maybe more. It's bound to have an effect.'

My Mum has been thoughtful about this then says: 'I think that it's very relevant because even when we were all a bit better off, and we didn't have to think about the wheat coming up in the summer, we really, really *did* because it didn't matter that some great, huge mega-acred farmer was doing it; someone was still doing it and still having that effect on the environment and on the Earth. Those things do need thinking about and I think that because it's a religion that's based very much on how you feed yourself, I think that has great relevance to people now. Society's changing. People are becoming so much more aware of how we feed ourselves and what we feed ourselves with and how much it costs and what it costs in terms of the environment; about things like GM produce.'

I wonder aloud: 'What would happen if it all went away? If nobody lit a fire at Beltane anymore? If nobody celebrated the harvests?'

Dad notes: 'It would be sad.' Then he adds with a touch of sarcasm: 'It would be the end of the world as we know it!'

Mum joins in with the same tone: 'The sun wouldn't come up in the morning!'

Dad continues with more seriousness: 'It certainly wouldn't for some people. I can say that hand on my heart. I don't know about you but I wouldn't want to be a part of a world like that.'

Mum agrees: 'A lot of people would be lost wouldn't they? They'd feel abandoned.'

And what about the things we've talked about, like remembering a skill that you didn't achieve through your own experience, or feeling a presence or other sensations at places like Rudston; do my parents think that would just go away? If nobody celebrated the turning of the seasons, would we stop feeling that turn? The magic we feel in a special place; if we stopped responding to that, would it no longer be there for us? When we jump over a fire at Beltane, this small ritual is rewarded in feelings of lightness and continuity; the destruction of problems and the focus to achieve our goals. If we stopped celebrating the fact that we are a part of the world, rather than just parasites sucking at its resources, will we lose all that the world, the universe, can give us in return?

After some thought my Dad decides: 'No, I don't think they would go away, but I think they would lose their relevance completely, because *people* have gone away at that point.'

Mum agrees: 'If people didn't have any connection to the Earth they'd just continue to destroy it until there was nothing left.'

Dad continues: 'That's what I mean: there wouldn't be any people left, physically.'

Mum concurs: 'People need that connection to survive; we're in a unique position on the planet where we have the ability to destroy it. We need to have things in place to counteract that.'

I wonder if, as a species, we need to make a conscious choice not to destroy our planet.

Dad disagrees with my wording: 'I don't think we need to make the choice as a *species*, I think we need to make the choice as *individuals*. If we say 'as a species' then we're passing the responsibility off to some nebulous being, rather like Christ or Allah, and we shouldn't, we should be taking responsibility for where we live ourselves.'

My Mum notes: 'That's the difference between us and other creatures: we have the responsibility. The buck stops here.'

Dad brings this back to Paganism: 'It's also the difference in the way a lot of religions are: I don't look at the Celtic heritage and Wicca so much as a religion, but more of an experience. It's an experience in which the individual really is encouraged to take responsibility, whereas with Christianity or Hinduism or Islam and others the individual isn't encouraged to take responsibility. I think the closest you get to a faith that does that is Buddhism.'

I don't think my Dad is trying to say that there aren't any responsible Christians or Hindus; of course there are many people from all faiths who have a massively positive impact on the world and those around them. How I interpret his words is thus: there are so many rules in most of the 'mainstream' religions, that when you are carving your path, you rarely decide for yourself what is right, and what is wrong. In most orthodox faiths there are strict rules about what you can and cannot do; these take away from you the stress of having to decide for yourself how to act or react in certain situations. This may be a good thing; if someone stops themselves murdering the annoying neighbour because of their Christian values, then the end result is one less dead body, job done! I know that personally, I would always rather know that I had the strength and character that I didn't want to kill that person anyway, and found other ways around the situation through my own merit, and perhaps despite the whispering of my bloodthirsty Celtic antecedents!'

Mum continues in this theme: 'I think that what the Celts have passed down to us in a lot of ways is their individualism; the sense that everybody's pretty much as good as everybody else; to do your own thing, which also may include being aggressive!'

Dad points out: 'We have to have ways of tempering that, so that there are some human beings left at the end of the day: to go and be aggressive with tomorrow!'

My Mum thinks about the idea of us tempering our aggressive tendencies and decides: 'That's what society is for, isn't it? Even the Celts, though they spent a lot of time fighting with each other and stealing from each other, they had enough of an idea of how to build a society to make sure they didn't just wipe each other out.'

According to the Book of Invasions, even when the Tuatha Dé Danann came and kicked Fir Bolg bottom, they did it in such a way that the Fir Bolg remained in Ireland. It was done in a way that if everybody stuck to their own bit of Ireland, everybody would be happy.

Mum adds: 'It's like the Pale, which was a later version of the same thing, where the Nordic peoples were confined to an area around Dublin, but that didn't last – they wandered and robbed and stole...'

Dad continues: 'But it meant that by law, you could be 'beyond the pale'. It basically meant you do what you like but if anyone catches you doing it and they object, they can kill you. It's just a way of sorting out society, saying that within this area, these are the rules you live by; in that area, well we don't care but somebody probably does. You need to go talk to them.'

Moving away from the subject of society as a taming influence for the wild Celt, I ponder another aspect of their culture: music. My Dad already mentioned he was influenced by the Dagda, and I point out that as well as being famous for his club and cauldron, he is also famous for his harp. My Dad agrees, and says our whole family has been touched by that aspect of Celtic influence.

This is not just a throw-away comment from my Dad here; he plays various musical instruments including stringed, wind and many 'early music' instruments, as does my Mum who also sings well too. My sister has a glorious voice, and my brother is one of the finest young guitarists and bass players I have ever known. I play guitar, mandolin, mandola, Irish whistle and keyboards and dabble with drums and percussion. I write songs in many styles and love to write poetry that I can then twist into music. I have written a fair few verses for ritual now too, and all of these tend to have a song-like quality, which lend themselves well to being spoken by many voices. The magic when a rite like this comes together, voices in unison, rising and ebbing in energy throughout; it feels like nothing else on earth.

I'm not saying all Celtic peoples were musical, but they obviously thought enough of music to wind it so deeply into their mythology; it must have had a great significance for them.

My Dad reiterates: 'It's one of those methods of reaching a higher plane of consciousness.'

Mum's view is: 'Irish people are very, very keen on their music and in fact arts in general. If you're a [published] writer and you live in Ireland you don't pay taxes. I think that comes from a culture that really values creativity, even now. There's so many Irish authors, poets and so on, and of course you've got to take into account people of Irish descent; there's masses of them.'

From music to words to names: when I was 18 I found out, from my Mum, that I had been given a Wiccanning naming ceremony, and given a Wiccan name as well as the name on my birth certificate. Both names, the legal one and the Wiccan one, had a firm root in my Celtic heritage.

Mabh is a slight (only slight!) modernisation of Medb, and my Wiccan name, Macha Levana, combines a Celtic goddess with a word that is either a Hebrew meaning of 'Moon' or a Roman goddess involved with childbirth. Macha, depending on what tales you read, is either one third of the triple aspect of the Morrigan, or somebody in her own right who cursed the entire male population of Ulster with a terrible weakness. My Dad is quick to point out that the Morrigan is only 'one third' of the triple goddess. I disagree, saying that again, it depends on the story. Badb, Macha and Nemain can be the three aspects of the Morrigan, but sometimes they are named as Badb, Macha and Morrigan. Nemain and Morrigan are both named as the Dagda's wife at differing points in Celtic mythology. Even Medb, my other namesake, has links to the Morrigan and her actions.

My Dad points out that there is such a jumbled mix of history and mythology for the Celtic people that it is so hard to decide who is who; who is real, who is fantasy, and which mythological beings are simply exaggerations of real heroes and villains at the time.

My Mum gives a good comparison: 'It's like Robin Hood isn't it. He lived in about six different places. So did King Arthur, come to that.'

My Dad points out: 'Well he would, because the literal translation is 'High King'.'

Mum continues: 'When you get all these stories about, say, Robin Hood, and he lives in all these different places, and he does all these different things; or King Arthur; it's almost like there were various folk traditions that gradually amalgamated into all belonging to the same one, more or less. A bit like Christianity has picked up so many different bits of Pagan religions and added them into itself. I imagine a similar thing's happened with Celtic mythology.'

Dad and I agree we are fairly convinced it must have; just like my idea of the Celts absorbing pieces of the cultures they interacted with during their travels across the continent. Plus many of the texts that have been put together have been taken from snippets and snatches of what scholars could find. Celtic history *and* mythology started off as an oral tradition and it wasn't until much later that people started to write things down. Scholars in the first few hundred years AD started to pick the bits back up and start tying them together. Around 1100 AD you get the Book of Leinster, or the first version of it, which is the first real attempt to tie it all together into the Book of Invasions timeline we recognise today.

Mum is quick to make a very good point: 'Picking it up from all these different sources you're bound to get different accounts of things. Look at any two witness statements given to the police about the same event. You're gonna get a lot of variation.'

My Dad is delighted: 'And you've just made the most interesting comment anyone could have made about that: witness statements. We're not talking about stories here; they're not stories: they're witness statements. These are stories of actual events.'

What an interesting conjecture. All we can wonder is how much these accounts were exaggerated; how much it affects the accuracy of the telling, the fact that they're put into prose and poetry for the purpose of entertainment. Which of course was done over and over again, changing and growing the tale each time. My Dad adds that with these stories it's not just a pinch of salt you need, it's the contents of a Siberian salt mine!

We'll see a little more discussion with my parents in the next chapter, and I hope this has highlighted not only some of the reasons I and my family have connected with our ancestors, but also how easy it could be for *you* or anyone else to find out more about what led you to where you are today. Ask the right questions, and let the answers lead you to more questions. Never be satisfied; keep searching, and learning more about yourself, as well as your forebears, as you seek.

Chapter Seven

Fingers Through the Veil –
Personal Experiences with the Fae

So who has actually met the fae then? Who can say they have stood shoulder to shoulder with the Tuatha Dé Danann and lived to tell the tale? Dramatic, I know, but I hope I've painted a picture so far of creatures or beings that aren't necessarily nice and certainly not people you want hanging round all the time. But their strength, loyalty and compassion can be drawn upon like wells of clear, refreshing water, when they choose to appear. I asked around and found a few people, as well as myself, who have had all too close encounters of the otherworldly kind, with a more than a hint of Celtic influence.

My friend Chris, the descendant of Cú Chulainn, told the first tale I'll relay, and I was actually present for this one, so can attest to everything that happened here. We were at a private camp for people of a Pagan persuasion, when somebody brought a fox in that had been killed by a local farmer that day.

In Chris's words: 'A fox was killed and somebody retrieved the body. The people at camp didn't want anything to go to waste so somebody wanted the tail and somebody wanted the pelt, and then they decided to eat the meat. The guy doing it decided to cook it, and knew he'd have to *really* cook it because it's a carnivore and we don't really eat carnivore. It was offered to me and I thought, whoa, hold on a minute, this cannot be real. I've read this story; there is no way that dog meat, any kind of dog meat, can pass my lips, even though I was offered it three times, by three different people. I thought whoa, I cannot believe this is happening. Is this a test? Am I stupid enough to fall for this? No, I'm not going to. That was one that made my skin crawl. I thought, 'You're getting a bit too close! Behave yourself! Stick it back in the books where it belongs! I don't need it in my life right now'. That was a scary one.'

I love the way Chris refers to his ancestor, Cú Chulainn, as getting a 'bit too close', as sometimes it can be like this; the feeling that you are under scrutiny, or under some sort of ancestral obligation, can sometimes be overpowering, and it makes you want to step back and close your mind and heart to it at times. It can literally overwhelm the senses, especially the first few times it happens. The supernatural is just that; the word means 'more than natural' which, let's face it, most of us translate as *un*natural and try to get as far away from it as possible especially when it scares us. However, if you do open yourself to it, and let the fear in, thus dealing with it rather than hiding from it, then I do believe you learn from these experiences.

I went on to ask Chris: 'As well as the geas not to eat dog meat, there was the social obligation not to turn down food offered, wasn't there?'

Chris: 'You cannot turn down a meal which is offered to you.'

Me: 'Because that was how they ended Cú Chulainn; he couldn't refuse the dog meat, so he ate it, which obviously broke his geas, which made him fall under a weakness, but I think you were safe to say no, because we have no such social obligation now.'

Chris: 'I don't know. Do we? Are we not still socially obliged to go, 'Oh thank you, I'll try a bit; OK, I've tried it, I don't like it'? Because it's the old adage, have you tried it, no, well don't knock it. Everybody else was like, 'Oh I have to try it, oh I don't like it'. How tempted was I to say, 'Oh well, I'll try it', and as soon as it would have passed my lips...'

Chris shudders at the thought of the possible consequences of breaking his ancestral geas.

Me: 'Maybe it's like you were saying before though, you've reached into that archive of history and thought, 'He felt obliged in the same way and look what happened. I'm going to risk the social spurning and not do the wrong thing'.'

Chris agrees that it's back to that flip of the coin thing; Cú Chulainn may have flipped tails and eaten the dog meat, but Chris flipped heads and chose not to. No one thought less of him for refusing the meat, and he didn't break his aeons-old geas, all because he knew the tale of what his ancestor had done, and how it had ended him.

Chris also had an experience at another place we are both familiar with – a modern day stone circle known as Sentry Circle in North Allerton, North Yorkshire. We've already talked about how the veil is a metaphysical barrier between this world and another world. Call it the next world, if you will, or a different plane. However you think of it, it is another realm of existence. Chris and I were talking generally about the relevance of Celtic belief in a modern world, when he told me this warm and heart pleasing story about a strange experience regarding his father, which again, I'll let him tell you in his own words.

'Another tale, which is not necessarily concerning the Fae or Tuatha Dé Danann: it was a couple of years ago; it was after my Dad died. We were up at Sentry [circle, Lenthor Farm]. When Dad did die, Fi [Chris's wife] saw him. I tried my damndest to see him but he wouldn't appear. Fi saw him twice. I took myself up to the circle, because I had a call. I can't remember what I was doing, but all of a sudden it was, 'Get your frikking arse up to that circle'. So I took myself off, and sat. When I started out, there was a chill, then the sun came out and filled up the circle. Then my Dad turned up. It was the briefest of conversations, and it was a case of, 'I'm alright, I'm happy, I've met Uncle Robert. It's brilliant here. Tell Izzy'; not, 'Tell your Mum' or, 'Tell my loved one' or, 'Tell my wife', none of that; it was just 'Tell Izzy' (her name's Isobel) 'I love her; there's no rush'. That was the message.

'Unbeknownst to me, I'd been up there for two hours. I left this planet; I left this plane as far as I'm concerned, so that was a beautiful experience. I think it was from that point onwards I thought Right, I'm gonna find out – because he did say it's brilliant here, he's seen Uncle Robert etc. etc. So I thought hang on then, I'm going to find out, what is this lovely place, and how are you able to come back when you're dead? It was then that I started really reading into the Celtic history and the Celtic magic. That's where I found out: it *is* another plane, just a step, that's all it is. It's a step through the veil. They are so close. It's... I wouldn't say unbelievable, because it is believable, but it's so comforting and... special I suppose.

'Not only that, but when my turn comes I have the choice to die, to carry on or – well, it's my choice. This makes life a lot easier because you don't fear death, because it's not there. It is not the nasty, nasty thing that people think it is. It's just a step through the veil. Getting back to your original question, is it relevant in this life? If everybody can take that attitude then yes, it is relevant, because then you will not fear death and you will live life to the full, knowing that you'll meet your Mum, your dad, your granddad, your great-great granddad; they're there. Unless of course you've taken the choice to be reborn, which is itself another beautiful thought. Once I cross over, I may have made the wrong choice – it's that heads and tails thing again. So I can say OK, I've made the wrong choice, I don't really want to be here, I think I'll go back and learn a little bit more.'

This is as clear an example as I have ever heard about not only being given a glimpse through the veil, or perhaps something coming through the veil to visit us, but also about a message being so clear and plain that it set someone on a path of discovery that would quite possibly change the course of the rest of their life. Chris's experience isn't necessarily unique in its otherworldly nature, but it's unique in its clarity and the clarity of purpose of the visit from the other side. It's wonderful to hear a tale when 'ghosts' come not with riddles, or confusion, but with clear messages of love and reassurance; to let us know they walk only the space of a heartbeat away.

So what about my own experiences? I've never been visited so directly by passed loved ones, although I do believe I have felt their presence, particularly at Samhain when I have invited them back. I have never seen a ghost or spirit so coherently that I knew what it was that I was seeing, but I'm pretty sure I have met the Morrigan. A bold statement to be sure, but the confidence I have that she is in my life leads me to believe this was the presence I was experiencing.

One occasion was during a ritual with several other people, around the time of the autumn equinox. We were honouring the Morrigan and how she brings strength and passion, encouraging ambition and fostering the drive to keep moving forwards towards one's goals. The ritual reached a point where the energy was flowing between myself and the other participants; flowing around all of us like we were cells in an electric circuit. There was this feeling of presence and of great power, but this power did not seem to come from within us. Almost immediately after recognising this presence, the physical sensations started. It actually felt like there were two hands upon my shoulder blades.

Suddenly I was enveloped with the impression of great wings beating behind me yet also wrapped around me. In a way it felt like I had wings myself; like something had sprouted from the area around my shoulder blades. I also couldn't shake the feeling that there was someone standing behind me; both keeping me safe yet somehow gently pushing me forward as well. The hands on my shoulder blades felt as if there were two people there, one to either side of me each reaching an arm across my back to touch next to my spine. I wonder if this was simply my mind explaining the invisible support everyone in the circle was lending; a physical manifestation of the energy we created. Or was this another way that the Morrigan was presenting herself to me, to remind me of her different aspects?

I can't say for sure, but even years later this experience is so vivid. The feeling it still evokes even now is wonderful and reassuring; reassuring because the almost overwhelming presence of this powerful being, while inspiring fear, also reminds us that if we are respectful we can go past the fear to a point where we can learn and be given strength. To keep moving forward, whilst honouring our past and listening to the guidance of our forebears; this is truly walking respectfully with our ancestors.

Chris gives me another couple of tales, one about an Irish sprite many will be familiar with, and one about something more sinister, which may indeed hail back to the original tales from the Irish Celts.

Again, in his own words: 'One tale is about my Mum. Mum is an Irish protestant, always went to church, but Mum and Dad had a secret side. As kids we didn't know what this side was. She'd know things that mums weren't meant to know and Mum and Dad would disappear once a month and go skinny dipping and get together with other adults, especially aunties and cousins. She still claims to this day that she's a churchgoer but I don't think so; she's a witch.

'One night she came in; we could hear her coming back up the alleyway, and she stopped, then 20 minutes later she came through the back door. We were like; 'What kept you?' She'd been talking to a leprechaun. Now had that been anyone else it would have been, 'You're pissed, you've had too many Mother, go to sleep, go to bed'. But not Mum. She told us the conversation that she had and the reason she had the conversation was because she recognised who or what she was talking to; through heritage, through the stories; she realised what to ask for and what not to ask for, because had she asked for riches, favours, etc.; well you know the old saying, careful what you wish for, for you'll get it.

'So none of that; so she stood and had a conversation, a civil, 'How are you doing? Are you enjoying yourself?' conversation. She didn't ask for any favours, didn't ask for any wishes or pots of gold; none of that crap. She just had a conversation just like she would do with anybody else in passing, and I believe that to this day, because Mum still believes it. She's 80 in January and she'll tell you the exact same story, without deviation, so it has to be true. So that was Mum's experience, and I suppose my experience with them as well.

'Another one: teenage years, in the bedroom, having a few bevvies, as you do. We were always aware of what lived up the woods; we didn't know what it was but we knew that something was there; the woods were different; things lived in them woods, not of the human. But we lived with it because we grew up with it.

'One particular night, as I said, sat in the bedroom, having a few bevvies, all of a sudden we heard this almighty, unearthly sound. It wasn't a scream; it wasn't a cry; it wasn't a shout. It was a cross between a cat getting its neck rung, a baby crying, a whistle blowing, a kettle boiling; it was all that and none, and it chilled you to the bone. It sent our flesh into goose bumps.

'[We asked]: 'What the hell was that?' Like fools we ran to the window to see what the hell was happening because it was right outside, and there was nothing but a wisp of smoke. That was it: a wisp of smoke. When it was passed we were screaming down to Mum, 'Did you hear that! Did you hear that?' 'Oh that was the banshee'. 'But that means you're gonna die!' 'No, that means *somebody's* gonna die. It doesn't mean you're gonna die. It just so happens that you may be that way inclined that you can hear them. Our family has nothing to do with them', is what she told us. '*Our family* has nothing to do with them. Don't worry about it. It's just unfortunately somebody, in this vicinity, will die.' So that was my personal experience with the Fae.'

I'm very intrigued by what Chris's mother meant by, 'Our family has nothing to do with them'.

Chris explains: 'The Banshee is attached to two, maybe three clans – I honestly can't remember. I think the O'Reilly's are one of them. They are specifically attached to them. So yeah, you can hear a banshee and get away with it. If you're not an O'Reilly or whichever of the clans it is, yes you'll hear the banshee if you're that way inclined, but she'll pass you by. What she's doing is saying, 'I'm here for somebody. Somebody is going to die tonight.' Unfortunately the one with ownership doesn't want to hear that! It all depends on your roots, but apparently the McCulloughs, descendants of Cú Chulainn, have got nothing to do with it. Maybe it's because of his association with the Morrigan, I don't know. But the banshee doesn't affect the McCulloughs.'

Although the Morrigan is not a banshee as such (although the term 'bean sí' simply means woman of the fairy hills) her cry was associated with the banshee; her war cry and the banshee's death cry seem to have very similar significance at times. Although at times she swore to attack Cú Chulainn, she also swore to protect him, to guard his death,[36] ambiguous though that statement is. Maybe the protection from the banshee is part of that legacy.

I return now to the discussion with my parents. We briefly touched on a few 'otherworldly' experiences, and how those can be connected to our ancestors, but have they had any personal experiences that are of a truly supernatural nature? And could they attribute these to beings from the Celtic or Irish mythology they show such an interest in?

My Dad seems a little unsure where to start with this: 'I don't know what to say there, because I think I'm not out of place in saying we've both experienced things that are not necessarily easily explained, but had a link into that kind of [Celtic] belief. Weird.'

Mum is a little more specific: 'We had a very strange tape recorded at one point, which was to do with the Morrigan and a banishing ritual.'

I recall that I have actually heard this tape when I was much younger. You can hear the voices of the participants and the movements around the room just as you would expect. Abruptly, in a totally different quality, as if someone had added an extra track on in a studio, there is another voice that says nothing I could comprehend. Indeed it sounded slightly garbled, as if something was trying to communicate on a frequency that didn't quite match our own. I remember when I heard this voice I was instantly covered in goose bumps. It had such an alien quality, but also, it seemed like a voice that was definitely trying to say something of import. It was a gravelly growl, animalistic and tied to some deep instinct that triggered fear and caution, but not terror; it wasn't a nightmare voice.

The strongest emotion it evoked in me was curiosity. I had a healthy dose of cynicism that this tape had not been tampered with, but I'm assured it was simply a standard tape deck with a record button and a built-in microphone, so if anyone had made the noises themselves they would have had to do it in a room full of folk who I'm assured were utterly shocked to hear this other-worldly voice when listening to it afterwards.

My Mum admits that the whole thing was very strange. I thought the sounds were totally incomprehensible, but my Dad disagrees, saying that when listening to the shapes of the sounds, it wasn't a huge stretch of belief to think that they were words, or the formation of words. None of us have any idea what caused this, or what the message, if it was a message, was trying to convey! So unfortunately, the most it did was assure us of *some* supernatural presence. But of course, you can look at this totally the other way: fortunately, it reassured us of a supernatural presence! I guess it all depends on your viewpoint.

Remember the sparkling sensation we touched on earlier?

My Mum expands on this a little: 'When we were in Ireland I remember when we used to go out of Dublin there used to be a lot of places where you get the little sparkles – you know the little sparkles? It's not just me then?'

I nod and my Dad confirms: 'It's not just you.'

My sister expresses bafflement at my Mum's statement.

Mum explains: 'When you're outside sometimes and you get a really lifted up feeling and you can see little sparkles in the air like there's little tiny... I can't really describe it! You've either seen it or you've not seen it!'

Dad exclaims: 'Rudston! That's a good example. We've both experienced something there.'

Mum is concerned that Rudston Monolith might not be a good example, as it's not anything to do with our Irish ancestry, but Dad points out that its origins are Celtic so there are links. Also, any experience like this is of interest to me; anything that shows we are still capable, like our Celtic antecedents, of recognising another realm of existence.

Mum tells me: 'That's a bit of a creepy place. It made us both feel very cold and weird.'

Dad concurs: 'If you want an experience, go there. It's not far. It's near Beverley is it? I'll find you a picture of it online. Just seeing a picture might actually spark a bit. It's one of those places where they've built a church on a Celtic site; it is rather obvious when you go there. It's called Rudston Monolith. It's a known Celtic site and it's probably even older. They just built the church around it. We've certainly had an experience there. I can't even describe it.'

Mum: 'Chilly!'

Dad: 'Yes! Like opening the door of a big fridge.'

Mum: 'You know sometimes you can walk into a place, an old place, and you can feel history? It's like that only just a bit too overwhelming.'

Dad: 'It's not like being slapped in the face; it's like someone jumping on your head from behind without warning you.'

Mum: 'It feels alien; it feels s like something you don't understand.'

I wonder if they have any idea why this is; what makes it feel so strange, so *different*.

Dad answers: 'I'm really not certain myself but I think the

whole environment must be saturated in experiences.'

Mum ponders: 'Maybe a lot of them [those experiences] are quite alien to us. Or it could even be the atmosphere caused by the fact that it's got a church round it that's dedicated to something quite different. It's hard to say but it definitely does feel quite odd.'

Dad urges me: 'You really need to pay it a visit sometime.'

Mum immediately thinks of another experience and looks to my Dad for detail: 'Where was that owl? The owl that led us somewhere.'

If you've read the chapters on the seasons, specifically about the winter solstice, then you can imagine how directly this resonated with me. If not, just pop back and read that section to understand why. That night, the longest night, trekking through the woods, with only wings to guide us in and out; it thrilled me to think that my parents had a similar experience.

Mum continues: 'I can't remember where it was, but I remember we found somewhere...'

Dad is racking his brains: 'I've forgotten now, and I'm still actively forgetting it for some reason. I get just to the edge of the memory and then it's snatched away.'

Mum tells me what she can: 'It was some sort of grove we found, but I don't remember *where* we were when we found it. There was an owl, a barn owl, and it flew down and it flew away from us. We followed it and found this grove, which was really quite interesting.'

Dad is aggrieved: 'I just can't remember where, and that's odd because I can usually draw a map of anything.'

How strange, the ability our mind has to snatch things away from us, even though we know the memory is in there somewhere. Perhaps we can infer that my parents' experience was *not* to be shared; it was for them and them alone.

Once, I had a very magical summer afternoon in a place that practically reeked of potential and power. Even though I felt in nature's grasp, it was so beautiful I couldn't resist getting my phone out and taking pictures; I immediately felt like I had brought an electronic intruder into a world that was not to *be* recorded; this time was for me and the universe and nothing else. The next day, my phone broke and all those photos were lost. I was upset because I wanted to go back to those pictures again and again, but it also taught me that some things are simply not for sharing. Some experiences are given as a gift to be treasured only by us; sometimes from within ourselves; sometimes from beyond the veil.

Chapter Eight

Sunset

So as the sun goes down on my exploration of people's experiences and opinions of their own Celtic ancestry, what's next? Well for you, I hope you've learnt something about how modern people can relate to an ancient culture, and at the very least you've been entertained with our stories, and maybe even inspired to find out a little about your own heritage. You may be thinking about your next steps forward into a world where you wish to connect to just a little more than you already have around you. You may be celebrating that which you have already.

For me there'll be a further voyage into the detail of Celtic culture, where such can be found. There are so many aspects that I find appealing. One in particular is the seeming absence of sexism. Tacitus observed in the year 100 that the Celts made no distinction between male and female rulers,[37] and the stories and legends we have touched upon in this book clearly portray both genders as strong, powerful, sexual and intelligent. This is refreshing when our own supposedly *modern* culture still directs its advertising towards women who stay home and do the cleaning and men who play video games and football. How nice to know that thousands of years before women started burning their bras, and guys were afraid to be seen as 'weak' for not enjoying sports, there was a culture that did not even comprehend why the genders should be segregated in this way.

I think the Celts understood that fundamentally women and men were *different*, but they also clearly believed that both were capable of greatness, and that being different does not make one gender less important or worthwhile than the other. It was just as much an honour to be a great sorcerer, sage or wise man or woman, as to be a fierce fighter, or a generous host. Maybe by retelling these tales we can make people today understand that one's gender should be an impediment to anything you do (or don't) want to do.

My friend Chris got his ear bent loads in the making of this book; while I still have him to hand, I ask him if he thinks the Tuatha Dé Danann will still have a presence in another thousand years' time.

He doesn't have to think about this long before he replies: 'Yes. Like I said before, it cannot die, it will not die, as long as we have fairy tales, children's stories, they have to live on. Like the tooth fairy: that's just a beautiful thing that you instil in your children, that a fairy will come along, take your tooth and leave you gold, silver or shiny baubles. Or in these days, a fiver! But that is just make believe as far as the child's concerned, but it's not! It's delving back into the Fae, the Tuatha.'

All these tales of exchanges and gifts (like the tooth fairy) are a metaphor for transformation. For anybody who is on a spiritual path, this should make sense: some of the voyage has to be about transformation, development, change and growth otherwise what's the point? Why would anyone make a journey with no goal at the end of it? Even travelling simply to *enjoy* the journey changes us in some way. We have to keep our senses open to the world around us, so that we don't miss anything along the way. That's when we realise that many of these so called fairy tales are *real*. When things in your life suddenly change, that is the story made manifest.

Chris comments on the serendipity of events; the things we can name coincidence and chance, and his own ideas on the purpose of any spiritual path: 'When things happen, how did it happen? Why did it happen? Once again, we're back to the heads and tails thing again. Why did I make that decision? If you were to look back and think *why* did I make that decision, what was there in my life, at that time, to make me make that decision;

nothing tangible. I had an inkling; I had a feeling; where did that come from? I just don't know. Did somebody visit you in your sleep? Did you have a dream? So that all stems back to the Fae, the Fir Bolg, the Fomorians, The Tuatha; because they have that ability.

'So yeah, in a thousand years time, they'll still be around; they will still be talked about. They need to be talked about, and they know that, because if they're not, they no longer exist, and they don't want that. They can't have that, and they've existed for thousands of years up to now so they're doing something right! So the simple answer to that one is, 'Yes'.

'You came up with a good one there: What's the point? I think the point is learning. The Buddhists call it enlightenment, so the Buddhists, like us, will live a life, learn, die, go off to a better place, think about what they've learnt, come back and try again. And that's exactly what we do. We live, we learn, we then pass through the veil, have a bit of a party, as you do, because we're Irish, contemplate what you've just learnt, the experiences you've had, then you go back and you do it a bit more.

'Unfortunately, the gods that be play a nasty little trick on us and remove our memory, so in the first part of your life you have to relearn what you learnt in a full life prior to that, which a lot of people do. There are a lot of very intelligent pre-teens out there, a lot of very intelligent teenagers who then go on to learn a little bit more. They in turn grow old, die, pass on; go over what they have learnt. Have I learnt enough? No, I'm going to go back and learn a little bit more. So the whole point of it is learning. If you can learn to live with yourself, that's when you can rest; that's when you can pass on.'

Chris came to his understanding of his Celtic roots partway into his grown life, after researching his family name and discovering his amazing heritage. I ask his opinion on how important it is to look after this heritage and the Celtic ways, the traditions, the festivals, the myths and legends; how important is it to keep them alive, and why? How does it benefit us, as a race, later down the line?

Chris is clear on this: 'It is important to keep them alive because it's *your* heritage, it's... it is *your* library of knowledge. It's what you need. You need to be able to delve into that library for info; you cannot come up to one of these decisions, these junctures that we talked about, and go blindly left or right. You have to go back to the library; your ancestors; the tales you were told by your dad and your granddad, and have a look. Get a bit of info, then make the decision, and like I said before whether it's heads or tails, that's the decision you're making, through your ancestors.'

So it seems to me that by doing this we are combining our own experiences with the experiences of those that have gone before us, to help us make a more informed decision at the juncture we have reached.

Chris confirms: 'Yes. So I think it's important to keep it alive, but on saying that I don't think it *is* the sort of thing that would dwindle and die. It was there centuries before we came along. It'll be there centuries after we go. It's not the sort of thing that dies and gets forgotten. It's instilled in people. Even if you're an Irish Catholic: 'That's a load of bollocks, I don't believe in that!' the point is you've heard of it; it's there, whether you believe in it or not. You'll tell the tales – 'Oh, have you heard this one? I don't believe it, it's a load of crap, but have you heard it?' So you'll tell your child, who'll make their own mind up; is it good or bad; am I indifferent? Do I believe it? But they'll tell their children. It's a tale that will go on forever. It won't be forgotten. That's my opinion.'

I guess this is only true as long as there are people alive who care about their ancestors and where they came from, even if this is a purely selfish need to riffle through the pages of history; for self-improvement, for knowledge, for education and for assistance in day-to-day life; to learn from the mistakes of those now either dead, or simply removed from us and now peering with curiosity through the veil.

My son, as he gets older, may share my passion for my Celtic heritage, but there is nothing to guarantee this, and of course I would never force this interest upon him, just as I will not force on him my 'religious' beliefs; my spirituality, for want of a better term. Indeed, I feel that to encourage it too much may drive him away from ever wanting to find out what came before, or why Mum is so into this weird stuff! If he decides that he is not interested in our Celtic heritage, then what is there to keep my words alive; the words of my mother and father, and the tales they passed down? Why will anyone keep our stories, if there is no one who cares to hear them?

I can only hope that, like my mother and father, future generations will suddenly hear the call of their ancestors and want to look back, to find the information; indeed, to delve into that library of experience from their ancestors and the tales and legends their ancestors told. They may change through retelling, just as the Book of Leinster is hardly going to be the same as the tales told by the Irish Celts themselves, but perhaps tales change because we need them to, because they need to fit in with our understanding of the world. They adapt to our own personal context. As long as the feats and heroism, the magic and mystery, the fantasy and the sheer super human magnitude of the Tuatha Dé Danann are not lost over the coming centuries, I think I will be satisfied.

Chris is right in saying that because much of the 'history' is in story form, it has a clear advantage, because stories are amazing: they are completely accessible by *anyone*. You don't need to have a particular belief system, or be spiritual, or have any link to Celtic heritage to appreciate the entertainment value in the stories and tales held within the Book of Invasions and related texts. Through translation, as we said before, they change, and grow, and maybe even lose something of themselves at times, but the story is what *keeps it alive*. And that gives me hope.

Appendix A

A Very Few Exercises for Those Interested in Magic with a Celtic Twist

Please don't try any of these exercises with the book out in front of you like an instruction manual. There is nothing in here that can end with your house being burnt down, so following my words 'to the letter' is not necessary. The reason I say this is because when you are doing any exercise such as the ones that follow (or indeed, any exercise at all), you must have a goal in mind. If you don't have a goal in mind, why are you doing it? To see what happens? Kind of a goal in itself, but not enough, I feel, for you to stay focused on the task at hand.

An age-old joke pops to mind here, 'Why did the chicken cross the road?' Although, 'To get to the other side' always seems a facetious answer, if that's what is necessary then 'Go Chicken!!' I say. If you at least have a goal even *this simple* in mind, and one of these exercises seems right to help you achieve that goal, please read and get the gist of what needs to be done. After that, put the book down and let your instincts and your own experience guide you. Remember, the whole theme of this book is being in touch with your heritage and how it has led you here; if you are performing these exercises exactly as I say they are to be done and not listening to your inner voice, you may miss some crucial insight into that bond with your ancestors.

Often your gut feeling can be a very reliable guide; trust it from time to time. If you follow a path of 'craft' or 'magic' you may want to add a great deal more than I have put here. I certainly won't instruct you about casting circles or addressing the quarters because to some this may be either incomprehensible or wholly inappropriate; if that's your thing (as indeed it is mine at times!) then all these exercises can be done within your own trappings of tradition.

Seeking the Ancestors

Although it's fun for me to talk about the Celts because they are my ancestors, they may not be yours. How do you reach your own ancestors? How does any of us? One simple way we can get an idea of how our ancestors understood life is to do the same things they did; celebrate the same festivals, perform the same rituals, and in some small way try to make ourselves like them. Whether this is contrived or natural to us, we cannot help but by these actions gain some insight into how our ancestors appreciated their lives and what was important to them. This insight may be small, and based on practical matters, or you may find a more complex emotional understanding of what actually drove your ancestors to act this way in the first place.

There are other ways to reach your ancestors and some remain untried by me; I have no knowledge to impart on 'past life' experiences for example, and communing directly with the dead as individual spirits is also beyond me, or at least not experienced by me thus far. But I have found that with careful observation, an open mind and a certain level of reception to the 'unseen', you can sense your ancestors around you, feel their influence within your lives, and even call upon them to give you aid and succour.

Ritual to Reach Your Ancestors

I was set this task by a cherished mentor some time ago and I was given a goal and a basic structure, and left to fill in the details myself. I suggest you do the same, as it's really important that this experience is personal to you. You may read my account and find it completely resonates with you, but you'll see from the objects I chose and the symbolism involved that this experience was deeply personal, so I urge you to make it the same. You may not want to cast a circle, or honour the cardinal elements. If this is not your thing then as I said in the intro to this section, don't do it: do your own equivalent. Whatever works for you will bring you closest to your ancestors and allow you to share a moment where space and time become meaningless, and you are a part of both what has gone before and what is yet to come.

The general idea is to make a space where you can be alone with your thoughts. You must make sure you will not be disturbed during this. Make family members aware that this is special 'you' time and this is your space. You can sanctify this space any way you like. Objects linked to your ancestors will help focus your mind on the task at hand. The aim is to let your mind, your consciousness, relax into such a state that it can almost drift back through your genetic memory, or through time, to find some link with your ancestors. You could use meditation to reach this mental state; what you're ultimately after is that feeling where you are almost in a dream state, but still fully aware.

Imagine how you feel just before you fall asleep; if you hear a noise or need to get a glass of water you are perfectly capable of dealing with these things, but you are also relaxed, with the mind drifting gently rather than stressing on any one particular thing. So you are in this space, mind relaxed and malleable, with thoughts of reaching your ancestors at the root of your goal. Because you have focused on this aim in preparation for this time, your relaxed mind should *naturally* gravitate towards this goal. Make a note of anything you experience; images, smells, even sounds. They could all have relevance. How do you feel? *Is* there a presence? Don't be discouraged if not.

Perhaps pick up one of the objects relating to your ancestors and think about it; why does it remind you of them? What is its significance? You could do this task as many times as you wanted, and in many different ways, but I think the key is to record anything you experience and crucially make a record of how you feel before *and* after spending time like this in this space. You may not have any startling epiphanies, but I would be very surprised if anybody did this task and remained entirely unchanged, presuming their mind was open to the experience. Here is an excerpt from my journal, to show you how I prepared for my first attempt at this; just remember if you attempt this, try not to copy my plan exactly. It must be personal to *you*.

From my journal:

I have decided that as it is to be completed before Yule, this weekend's new moon feels like the right time; partly because the original rite [I had delayed it due to illness] was to be at new moon, and partly because new moon is a time for starting things, for sowing the seeds of something, and I feel that is what I am doing here; I am beginning, or renewing, a relationship with the ancestors I cannot see.

I will cast a circle. This is because although I will be talking to my ancestors, I don't know what else they will bring, purposefully or otherwise, with them, and I want to protect myself and my house/family. I will perform the ritual at sunrise; symbolism of a new start, hope, light, and wanting to learn. I will use traditional elemental symbols: salt, fire, incense and water, and at each elemental point I will put something that pertains to my ancestry or heritage.

I have no words written as yet, and I may just go with whatever feels right at the time. I want to introduce myself, and where I am from. I want to welcome my ancestors and hope they are watching. I want to thank them for the things I have gained from them: my skills, my intelligence, my appearance; all is based on my ancestry and I want to acknowledge that although I am a self-made woman in my own personality, I am also partly the result of centuries of other lives. I want to state my intent: to be closer to my ancestors, to understand their lives better, to learn more about them and how it can benefit me and my family, particularly the traditions and crafts of my family throughout the ages. I think in a time when self sufficiency is becoming more and more important, looking to the past to see how things were done becomes equally crucial.

I will spend some time in the circle to see what I feel and what I sense.

I will close it down thanking *all* for their presence, including the spirits that naturally reside here, and those that may have come from afar drawn by my working. I will give them leave to depart and ask for the blessings of my ancestors. I will close the circle and again sit within the area afterwards to feel the difference and to chill out.

I will spend the rest of the day with my immediate family, and have a big bloody meal!

So what *was* my ultimate goal? To perform a ritual to honour and respect my ancestors, with the hope that I would be able to commune with them in some way; to feel their presence, or to invite them to share this space and time with me. The idea was to create this sacred space that they could visit temporarily, then safely dismiss them and as previously mentioned, note any learning, feeling and afterthoughts. To keep my ritual in keeping with similar ones I had been a part of at the time, I cast a circle: a sacred space within a boundary separating the sacred, magical area from the everyday world. I performed a calling of quarters and cardinal elements. I tried to find objects that were a direct link to my past and ancestry.

I used an ornamental egg of my grandparents, which is beautiful and fragile. I placed this at East, as it is the symbol of new beginnings which always makes me think of mornings and the rising sun. I also used a beautiful ebony brush belonging to my great grandmother, who I never met. This was placed at North. As a symbol of a mother and all the mothers I have never met, it reminded me of the element of earth, often regarded as a great mother. At South I hung a sword which was a replica of one used by my ancestors in the English Civil War. This I used as a symbol of fire; the fires of the forge where it was made, the fires of war and the fires of creativity and passion. I had a picture of one of my supposed Celtic forebears, the Morrigan, at West; my Wiccan name is for one of her aspects and it seemed appropriate to honour this. West to me represents water as a river of life; a journey through time that I have always been on, and a river that I now wished to swim back up in order to see what came before.

So this seems quite an elaborate set up; I can tell you now if I did it again I would not stress so much about the detail. To be honest, I was *so* nervous about getting this right I spent more energy on the preparation and almost missed the point: this is as much for *me* as it is about honouring my ancestors. Make sure if you do this task that you are comfortable and relaxed, because then you will get the best results. So what were my results? Here is my report to my mentor:

I can't tell you that I felt anyone in particular; however I did feel that something was telling me to wait, and be patient, and something would come to me. After closing the circle I felt a little uneasy if I'm honest; I think perhaps this was just a comedown from the nerves as I was really jittery beforehand. Just over a week later, at first quarter, I went for a walk in the twilight, and was overcome by feelings of nostalgia; not the soft fluffy kind but the sharp pointy kind, when you know you need to remember something. It was like my brain was trying to make me feel something I had felt only at one time or place before.

After a bit of 'what's that in my peripheral vision' it came to me – the feeling I was having was the feeling I have had only at a couple of places in my life, places I have always thought of as magical for one reason or another. I decided that after this realisation perhaps I should go visit these places, and see what they mean to me now. When I thought about it later, I thought maybe this was my ancestors speaking to me, trying to get me to understand how I have come to be the person that I am... what do you think?

Anyway, after this, I walked home, and three odd things happened. Firstly, there were loads of dogs going mental; some started fighting, then ones that usually bark when you walk past just stared. Then there was a strong smell of coal (I live in a smokeless zone), then finally there was a shadow on the floor but I became convinced it was a dark pool of water and couldn't get the image out of my head, and as I walked around it I was covered in goose bumps which lasted pretty much all the way home.

It took me about a year to visit all these places I referred to; these places of magical significance. Doing so has brought something into my life that I can hardly describe; the comfort of knowing that I am near places where the world is a little different; places where I can be alone with my thoughts with no fear of discovery; places that are wild in winter and joyous in summer. I truly feel that all this stems from that first task I performed, and that this is the gift my ancestors have given me.

At Imbolc

There are many crafts associated with Imbolc and lots of them are associated with Brigid. One is the making of Brigid's Cross out of grass or rushes. Of course, the cross is associated deeply with Christianity these days, but the original simple, symmetrical crosses represented the sun. Brigid is the goddess of fire and the returning spring, so it seems appropriate to make these 'Sun Wheels' for her. If you learn how to make one of these, you can turn it into a little bit of a 'bonding' exercise; if Brigid resonates with you, think about her as you make the cross. Why are you doing this? Is it for her? Is it for you? What does it represent? Think about the turning of the seasons; this is one way for you to get closer to the spinning of the earth. Can you feel the change? Is that smell of damp earth on the air the promise of spring?

Another tradition is to create a small space, like a box or a bag, with three compartments. It could even be a piece of paper divided into three sections. You need three, divided areas because you want to think about a very common theme in spirituality:

what was, what is and what shall be. Essentially you are going to make one of those spaces your past, one your present, and one your desired future. Beyond this you have free rein.

Some people use the first box to leave something behind them. They may write down the name of someone who has been a thorn in their side that they have finally decided to be rid of. Perhaps a small toy plane goes into a box, celebrating that they have overcome their fear of flying. Correspondences could be used; supposing a piece of hazel wood means clever words, it could signify the end of an argument with someone, or a peace. It doesn't have to be literal; it's whatever means something to the person making it. The second box is about what's happening now; again, this could be something you're celebrating, something you're hoping will pass or simply an observation. You could even place something on behalf of a friend; a hope for them to see better days perhaps.

The final box or section is basically a wish for the future; a *prayer* I guess. It can also be a boast; a promise to do something amazing. Or it could be a long-term goal that you are simply moving one step closer toward. The box is sealed; the paper is folded; the bag is tied. No one needs to know what is inside but you and Brigid; ever present at Imbolc. Keep it for a turn of the moon. Think on what you placed in it and why. And finally, when these four weeks have passed, dispose of it. Many folk I know bury it. I burned mine, but please be careful with fire! Do it outside away from buildings if you are going to do this and if you don't know what you are doing, then choose another way.

Now that you have disposed of your thoughts and desires, they are, once again, left simply with you and whatever you have pledged them to. In my tradition, they have been pledged to Brigid, in the hope that she will help the goals come to fruition and accept the thanks for things that have already gone well. Just remember: no one is there to do your work for you; any goals or commitments have to be kept up to by *you* and no one else. The 'gods' may make things easier for you and move obstacles out of your path, but not if you are inactive or lazy. This exercise is more about focusing your own mind and heart on what is truly important, helping you prioritise and plan for the year ahead.

Ancestral Feast

At Samhain, as discussed earlier in this book, it's important to honour those who came before you (or beside you, the time aspect isn't really important) and influenced you in some way. This may be an ancestor, a teacher, a student or even a pet. Anyone who inspired you at all can be honoured here. Find a symbol of that person, or those people. A picture is best but not necessary; for my grandparents I have a dagger that is part of a set that was used when they did English Civil War re-enactments, so it was a part of something that they loved, and thus to me it will call to their happy memories. Display the picture or symbol somewhere prominent with a candle lit as the sun goes down on the 31st October.

Provide your chosen person or people with some form of sustenance that will mean something to them. If you know them well enough, their favourite food is a good idea if possible. One year, I made my Nana a cup of tea just like she used to have. If you have friends who want to join in, you can lay a table with several places for all the 'ancestors' who will be joining in. The idea is, your people will come and enjoy the space you have created for them, pleased and happy that you have remembered them and the things they enjoy.

There is nothing more to it than that really. You are celebrating the people that mean something to you, and hopefully they are celebrating your life and achievements and are proud that you choose to honour them. When the time has passed, simply clear the feast away with respect and thank them for their presence. Again, if you want to record feelings and experiences, this can be very valuable, but this is also a time to simply be; to exist in the space you have created, and enjoy your family, your *whole* family to its fullest.

Burning the Dross

To be done at Beltane. Write down all the things you want to get rid of. These don't have to be physical things; they can be self-doubt, a crappy job or biting your nails! Take your time; don't try and be clever, just be honest. If you think your idea is too simple, you may be over thinking it. If all you can think of is 'that horrible top in the back of the wardrobe' then lucky you, you have a pretty ace life and your problems are easy to fix! One very Celtic ideal I have come to embrace is 'don't go looking for problems that aren't there'.

Write them down; really focus on the idea of getting that problem or item or habit out of your life. Screw the paper up or fold it up, and throw it on the fire. Yes, you need a fire for this one. If you have no place to safely set a fire, then use a candle flame but *please* be careful, if you are unsure at all have a bowl of water nearby to douse the burning paper in if necessary.

That's all. Enjoy the rest of your Beltane, don't give those problems another thought for that day. Then if they crop up again the next day, remind yourself that you have *committed* to getting rid of them, and do whatever it takes to be true to that commitment. Take that top to the charity shop. Get some nail biting deterrent. Change jobs. Learn a new skill. Leave the damaging relationship. Whatever it takes, be it small or large: it's up to you. Just make sure that at the next Beltane, you are writing different things on the pieces of paper. That's when you know that you have succeeded; you have worked magic within your own life.

Appendix B

Celtic Inspired Correspondences

Trees

Trees and different woods certainly seemed to have special significance for the Celts as they appear in their tales as magical tools and places of significance many times over. There is also a great deal of modern interest in the Celtic tree calendar, but research shows that it is incredibly unlikely any Celtic people ever followed such a calendar, mainly because this calendar is a fixed, 13-month calendar, and the Coligny Calendar suggests a more fluid method of timekeeping was used, following a combination of a solar year and lunar months.

The tree calendar is entirely modern and any source it uses relating to trees and druidic worship of them probably only dates back as early as the 14th century. However, it is certainly interesting to see the Gaelic names taken from the Ogham symbols, even if the timekeeping aspect is not directly related to the Celtic people themselves. I will include this 'calendar' as a point of interest here, with an aim to look at how each of these trees actually popped up from time to time in Celtic mythology.

Beth (Birch) December 24 to January 20
Luis (Rowan) January 21 to February 17
Nion (Ash) February 18 to March 17
Fearn (Alder) March 18 to April 14
Saille (Willow) April 15 to May 12
Uath (Hawthorn) May 13 to June 9
Duir (Oak) June 10 to July 7
Tinne (Holly) July 8 to August 4
Coll (Hazel) August 5 to September 1
Muin (Vine) September 2 to September 29

Gort (Ivy) September 30 to October 27
Ngetal (Reed) October 28 to November 24
Ruis (Elder) November 25 to December 22

December 23 is not ruled by any tree for it is the traditional day of the proverbial 'Year and a Day' in some early courts of law, which is still cited in some legal circles today.

Birch: Also known as 'Lady of the Woods'; I had never heard of this nickname until recently but have always found this tree to give off a very feminine energy. There is a particularly beautiful piece of woodland near where I live which is mainly oak and birch, and it really does feel like you are surrounded by grisly old men and wise, slender women. Birches generally get their leaves a little time before other trees, depending on the local water table, and as such are associated with birth, renewal and new beginnings.

Birch twigs have been used for the business end of besoms (broom sticks) for centuries, and the magical association there is obvious; the few references I have found in Irish literature referring to brooms nearly always refer to 'birch brooms'. In Buile Suibhne (Suibhne's Frenzy),[38] the protagonist describes the birch as smooth, blessed, melodious and proud. One of the wonders of Clonmacnois is a great giant appearing in a freshly dug grave, surrounded by brooms of birch (presumable meaning birch twigs or bundles of birch twigs), so the birch here seems to be associated with mystery and the unexplained.[39] Birch wood is used today to make some kinds of plywood as it is strong and stable. The sap can be used to make wine, and the leaves are a fantastic diuretic.

Rowan: This is an enormously powerful tree according to many sources. Cú Chulainn's fateful meal, the dog meat that causes his geas to be broken, is cooked upon rowan spits, indicating the use of harmful magic *or* perhaps the inevitability of his fate.[40] Conversely rowan wood is also used traditionally to ward off and protect from evil magic. In 'The Rowan Tree of Clonfert' the rowan tree on the hill is the protector of Goll, keeping him alive with but a few of its berries, and when Goll leaves its protective shelter, although he fights bravely, he is slain and is laid to rest in the hollow of the hill beneath its roots.[41] The Metrical Dindshenchas tell us that Eochaid was banished into Leinster for setting Crinna, son of Conn's, head upon a rowan stake.[42] Rowan berries are nutritious and make a wonderful jelly (tried and tested!) and are very attractive to birds. Do *not* eat them raw though! Rowan wood is very dense and because of this is popular in the making of wands, staves and staffs. I love the rowan tree because it's so colourful; the dark green of the leaves followed by the striking colours of the berries which can be anything from gold to deep red. I add the berries in incense to add a male aspect if required and also to represent the sun or fire.

Ash: Strongly associated with protection, this tree was thought to have grown originally under the sea, and as such carrying a piece of the wood offered protection from drowning. Please don't try this at home (or at sea)! The tree is also associated with divination. The tree was so sacred, often people refused to cut it, even when needed for firewood. According to Keating's History of Ireland, when the Tuatha de Danann were at war with the Syrians, the Syrians thrust ash stakes (although in another version of the same tale it is the Philistines with hazel pegs) through the dead bodies of their fallen enemies to stop them returning to life through the power of necromancy... by turning them into worms! I wonder if this was literal, or a turn of phrase meaning that they were immediately rotted.[43] So it seems that ash not only protects from magic, but counteracts with its own innate magic.

Ash is still used for wands today (apparently an ash wand

with spiral decoration, dating back to 100 CE, was found in Anglesey) and sellers of these items claim that it represents the cycle of birth and death. Witches' brooms or besoms often utilise an ash pole although this traditional tool also tends to be made from whatever strong and slightly flexible wood is locally available for the producer. Suibhne tells us the ash is a baleful tree and hand weapon to the warrior,[44] possibly indicating that this tree was used for spears or similar, which makes sense as our common name 'ash' actually comes from an old English word for 'spear'. Today ash wood is used for a variety of purposes including musical instruments and smoking food, showing how versatile it is. Ash seems to me to be the bridge between practicality and spirituality; in the Celtic world it was used as a weapon and for sorcery; force and guile. The ash represents flexibility and adaptability to different situations.

Alder: Related to the birch, the alder is easily identified by its catkins; round cones for the male ones and beautiful, trailing flowers for the female. The wood is hard and even, and as such is ideal for making musical instruments, an attribute exploited by Fender who have been using alder wood to make some of their most famous guitars since the 1950s. In Celtic mythology, Celtchar uses an alder log to kill the Dun Mouse, a great hound that has become wild and dangerous.[45] According to The Yellow Book of Lecan, Cormac mac Cuilennain brought a little alder to Inis Cealtra, which was then blessed so it grew apples. Alder is one of the woods that the 'wizard doctor' in Aislinge Meic Con Glinne advises MacConglinne to use to cure gluttony.[46] Although this story is a bit silly, it shows that the woods mentioned in this dialogue (also oak and ash) are associated in tradition with magic and healing; the author has included these woods as part of the magical cure to enhance the mystical nature of the conversation between MacConglinne and the doctor.

Alder loves to grow near water or in swampy areas and as

such can be associated with solitude or secrecy, as hiding among the alders means few will come searching for you unless they are prepared to get wet feet! I love the way the male catkins look like miniature versions of their parent: like tiny alder trees themselves. They often find their way onto my autumn altars as a beautiful decoration and tiny offering.

Willow: The Gaelic word saille means 'near water' which makes sense as this tree loves water and can be found alongside streams and lakes all across Britain. The wood is supple and has many practical uses, including basket work. Even when a stem seems dead, plant it and see what happens a year later – willow takes many seasons to dry properly and will return to life with just a little moisture and food!

Willow bark is a natural painkiller and one of the ancestors of our modern aspirin. Willow is associated with magic and fairies, and tales of folk disappearing for a year and a day, though it seems but a day has passed for them.[47] A rather wonderful story is of a youth who is crippled by secret knowledge of the king's deformity, and is sent by a druid to a crossroads, whereupon he tells the secret to a large willow tree which takes the burden away, healing him completely. When wood from the willow is used to fix a broken harp, the harp plays a song about the deformity of the king. When the king hears this, he realises he had nothing to be ashamed of, and openly reveals his deformity and no longer requires secrecy from anyone[48]. So willow not only heals the body, but the mind; here it soothes a proud king's self-esteem, to the benefit of all.

Hawthorn: Hawthorn is widely regarded as a sacred plant in many traditions, and in some modern Pagan paths it is referred to as a goddess tree. The gorgeous, creamy blossoms are known as may blossom and indeed, usually start to decorate our hedgerows at the start of May in England – sometimes a little later, but sometimes a little earlier depending on the season. If the flowers are available, I use them to decorate the house at Beltane.

Apart from being held sacred, they smell amazing; pungent, sweet and redolent of the changing season. The berries are small and red and birds love them; in the hawthorn and bramble hedgerow near our house the wrens, blackbirds, tits and thrushes squabble just as much over the 'haws' as they do over the juicy blackberries. Medically they are used to aid with heart conditions and as well as being recognised by herbalists for centuries they are also being tested for possible use in 'conventional' medicine. Please don't eat them without advice from a professional as they can cause cardiac arrhythmia!

The wood is very hard and while long stems aren't too common, it being quite a shrubby plant generally, if you find a long enough piece it makes a wonderful staff. In The Book of Ballymote there is a description of poets being judged to see whether their satire is in the wrong, or if the king they are mocking is in the wrong to refuse the satire. They have to face the kingdom in question with a hawthorn at their backs and each holds some of the hawthorn along with a 'slingstone', presumably meaning a stone the size of which was suitable to use in a sling. Once they had read aloud lines from their poem, they placed the stones and pieces of the tree at the base of the hawthorn, and if they were in the wrong the earth would swallow them up. Quite fantastic obviously, but it's interesting that the judge of this situation seems to be the tree itself, indicating a strong association with justice.[49]

In a similar vein of lawfulness, hawthorn is used across the British Isles as a natural boundary between farms and other spaces of wide, flat land, and it is perhaps this notion of it being a marker of boundaries that has given it such a magical reputation. We've already discussed that magic occurs at the edge of things, where choices are made and paths are taken;

where a whole other world is almost visible behind a veil of dreams. The thorns of this beautiful shrub have deterred trespassers for millennia, and are a natural, physical protector. It's only a small step to take this attribute into the metaphysical realm, and see the thorny plant as a protector of all boundaries, 'real' and otherwise.

Oak: There is speculation that the term 'Druid' is possibly derived from the Gaelic word Duir (or Dair), which is the Ogham letter representing oak. Oak trees are famous all across the world for reasons ranging from royalists hiding amongst their branches (The Proscribed Royalist, 1651 by John Everett Millais) to actually owning the land they have grown upon (the tree that owns itself in Georgia.) Specifically in Celtic mythology, the oak was the tree that Eochaidh hid in to shoot and kill Niall with his bow.[50] *Eo Rossa, Eo Mugna* refers to the great 'Oak of Mugna', but in *Mag Mugna* the Tree of Mugna seems to be describing a great oak anyway – with fruit of acorn, nut and apple; perhaps they are referring to galls and oak apples?[51] A story of Conchubhar's death tells us that he attacked an oak wood in a great rage, causing the 'ball' stuck in his head (it was actually someone's brain that had been launched at him with a sling – gross!) to become dislodged, giving him brain damage and killing him.[52]

The oak seems to be associated with themes of great change, particularly involving royalty. In (some) modern Paganism, including that which follows Celtic roots, the Oak King is the King of Summer, born at the winter solstice and growing in strength until the year reaches the summer solstice, where he is at the peak of his power but then starts to wane, as the crown is handed to the newly born Holly King. This is a nice, very visual representation of the ebb and flow of the seasons, and the oak tree does seem very masculine in many ways; old oak trees do have a habit of reminding one of gnarled, old men; or is that just me?

Oak is very hard, very strong and has been used historically for everything from 'Viking' long boats to sherry barrels. The acorns, as well as being gorgeous and decorative, are used to make a kind of coffee, and the bark can be used for tanning leather. Humans utilise so much of this tree, it's no wonder we have revered it throughout the centuries. For me, finding an oak leaf in autumn or winter is a reminder that change is always around the corner, and although things fade and die, there is always the potential for them to rise again.

Holly: The holly is an evergreen tree with leaves ranging from dark green to bright yellow and gorgeous red berries. We very quickly think of Christmas or Yule when holly is mentioned, and there is a long tradition of bringing greenery into the house at the coldest time of the year. Holly is one of the more beautiful examples of this as it really needs no trimmings or enhancements; it *is* the decoration. Holly is usually quite prickly and a full tree of the thorny leaves can be very dangerous. Cú Chulainn was forced to fight one of his foster brothers, Fer Báeth, and tried desperately to talk Fer Báeth out of the fight. Cú Chulainn left angrily; not looking where he was going, he stepped in a holly so sharp it cut him to the bone. He uprooted the bush in a rage and cast it over his shoulder, killing the unfortunate Fer Báeth. In the same text our hero comes across a charioteer cutting holly branches to make chariot poles, and later Medb's warrior Nath Crantail attacks Cú Chulainn with nine spits of charred and sharpened holly. Cú Chulainn simply hops along the tips of the spits as they are thrown at him then runs off to find his evening meal![53] Suibhne refers to the holly tree several times in his story as a sheltering tree, and at one point he is surviving only on water, acorns and holly berries[54]. It's no wonder he was in a frenzy; the berries have a similar effect to caffeine, and eventually become very toxic. In one version of The Wooing of Etain, Midir's eye was taken out with a spit of holly.[55]

From all these examples it seems safe to assume that holly was widely cut for weapons, vehicles and a variety of other uses by the Celts. Holly today is still common all over the British Isles and is very hardy, and as mentioned previously, is one half of the dual king of the year for those Pagans (and others) who follow this belief. The Holly King is born at midsummer, the summer solstice, but does not start to really rule supreme until after the autumn equinox, when night outweighs the light. I always felt that the Holly King had a bit of an unfair advantage, because he is green and lush all year around, whereas the Oak King loses his green mantle by October, not to retrieve it until well into spring. But how could we have a green lord of the wild, wintry wood, without turning to the endless magic of the evergreens?

Hazel: Hazel leaves and nuts have been found in burial mounds (for example the early Bronze Age cemetery found at Hengistbury Head near Bournemouth), suggesting straight away *some* significance to the culture at the time. This is backed up by the fact that the hazel appears frequently throughout tales of the Celts. To join the Fiann, or Assembly of Uisneach, one of the tests was to stand in a pit armed with only a shield and a hazel staff as long as the warrior's own arm. The applicant would then have to survive, unharmed, an onslaught of nine other warriors hurling spears at him.[56] Conaire Mór lives in a 'hazel-abounding land' according to Tadhg Dall Ó Huiginn[57] and the amount of times this same poet uses hazel trees to indicate beauty, lushness and even to emphasise reproach towards dishonesty is quite astounding.

It's impossible to say whether this is the 16th century poet's own whimsy or not, but most poets write for their audience at some level, so it is probable that he included the hazel this frequently because it *would* resonate with his readers, and enhance the mystery and beauty of his words.

So here we have the hazel representing strength, protection, initiation; then beauty and wonder, even truth. The hazel is also associated with magic, and certainly today many magical supply shops carry hazel wands, often utilising or mimicking the twisty, even spiral patterns hazel branches can grow in. The Celts were quite taken with spiral patterns, as can be seen from their artwork, particularly that in La Tène style, so it is quite possible the twisty branches of the hazel tree appealed to their artistic senses as well as their practical ones. The theme of magic and therefore wisdom is continued in the Metrical Dindshenchas, where the hazel is the 'poet's music haunted' tree.[58]

In The Táin, the Meic Árach think that using hazel will allow them to kill Cú Chulainn, but unfortunately (for them) he is too powerful. Later, Mac Roth the messenger carries a staff of white hazel which indicates to Cú Chulainn that, even though Mac Roth is armed, he has come to parley, not fight.[59] I am unsure whether the hazel here is representing the peace of the parley, or the words of the messenger, but looking at the aforementioned associations with poetry, music and wisdom, I lean more to the latter; the power of words. In Táin Bó Regamna when Cú Chulainn encounters the Morrigan in disguise, her companion is clothed in red with a two-forked staff of hazel upon his back. They are claiming to be poets at this time so again the hazel, to my mind, is representing the power of words. Morrigan actually says she is 'skilled in spells of satire' proving, to me, that the power of words was highly respected and even revered in this culture.[60]

Vine: Celtic art in La Tène style (such as the Turoe Stone in Bullaun, County Galway) often contains vines and tendrils (or patterns based on these) as decorative devices. This influence was probably inspired by the Mediterranean areas that the Celts may have travelled through. Vines always make me think of the Greek pantheon more than any other; Dionysus revelling in the ecstasy of the grape harvest and the anticipation of intoxication, representing freedom, the unexpected and the mysteries of life and death. The vine I guess is a catalyst for this; the grape, as wine, reduces our inhibitions and allows us to see things in a different way – not always for the better, but it is about change and realisation.

In Owen Óg MacSweeny the metaphor of children being extensions of a vine is used extensively. Twins are described as two stems from a single vine, and later as two vine groves from a single root.[61] The idea that children are the fruit of a dynasty and, as such, can be sweet or go bad is a powerful idea. It is in the same vein that wine is a tricky mistress, and can make one either jolly or maudlin; the vine perhaps being change and growth with the reminder that change is not always for the good.

Grape vines aren't too common in Ireland (or most places in Britain) because of the climate, so if we were to think of an alternative perhaps we would look to the bramble; dark green leaves, climbing, clinging branches and delicate flowers that transform into delectable fruit that, just like the grape, make a beautiful wine. It is appropriate, therefore, that the vine 'month' starts at the beginning of September; the final days of the blackberry picking season. Though the Celts would have most likely had no such named month, they would certainly have been gathering fruit at this time, and it's comforting in a way to think that when you are elbow deep in brambles, purple stained and prickled, your ancestors from thousands of years ago were probably doing the exact same thing.

Ivy: Not really a tree, but as it so often grows up and around trees perhaps it was thought of as a tree in its own right, or perhaps the Celts simply recognised and respected the symbiotic relationship the ivy has with trees. Again, it is often used as decoration in pieces of Celtic art, the tendrils and palmate leaves of ivy speak of beauty and delicacy, with an inner strength and awareness. Although it clings to and often takes some life from that which it grows on, it rarely (if ever) takes too much. Most trees (in Europe) are not harmed by ivy growing up them, and the ivy flowers and fruit encourage bees and other pollinating insects, even providing one of their only food sources in winter. Kohl speaks at length about the ivy covered bridges and buildings in Ireland and even goes so far as to say some of the buildings would crumble if it were not for the ivy holding them together.[62] So clearly the Irish climate is great for ivy and it would no doubt have been very present in our Celtic ancestors' lives; a bit of a contrast to the aforementioned grape vine which led us back across Europe to find the original influence for this plant's mystical allure.

Ivy is often used in conjunction with holly as a household decoration around the winter solstice. This is simply because of one fact: ivy is evergreen. Like the holly, its leaves remain green and glossy all year around. For this reason, it represents the return of spring, the life hiding in the frozen ground during winter, and the continuing change of the seasons. It reminds us that even in the darkest of times, there is hope, life, and the knowledge that what we need *does* return at the time it is needed.

Reed: I was always confused at this inclusion as obviously (to us) reeds are *not* trees, but it is possible that they were once considered so. Reeds do often have a large root base, just like trees do, and the clumps of stems sometime may appear to be one thick stem, but even so they still do not compare to the oak, ash, hazel and others; there is no splitting of limbs into boughs and branches and the leaves are more like grass than the leaves of trees. The reed was used to make musical instruments so it is possible that the Celts who travelled across Europe remembered that Pan played pipes made of reeds, and associated them with the divine and magical accordingly.

The reed is also associated with wisdom and knowledge through study, probably because reeds could be used to make pens; the Celts of course are *not* known for their writing skills so it's unlikely this association was formed until later. Reeds and rushes were used to line the floors of building and homes; clean reeds thrown upon the ground for a visitor showed honour and respect.[63] Reeds are also used to make thatch, and it is reasonable, based on buildings found in excavations of Iron Age sites, that at least some Celts would have lived or worked in buildings with thatched roofs, so reeds here become a symbol of architecture, craft, self-reliance and security.

Elder: Medicinally the bark is an anti-inflammatory, the berries are anti-viral and anti-catarrhal and particularly effective against chest infections. The flowers are very diuretic and make a great eye wash and both berries and flowers make an astonishing wine. This tree is another 'goddess tree' and you can still see evidence of people's reverence for it, in sights such as a newly tarmacked road which has been carefully laid around an ancient elder. Ever since I was a child I always knew it was bad luck to wilfully damage an elder tree unless it was to the tree's benefit e.g. pruning.

The branches can be hollowed out easily, as they contain only a pith-like substance. They make an excellent tool for breathing air into a fire, to bring embers to life. The elder is associated with banishment, protection and the gates to the other realms. Again it is a common hedgerow plant and appears at the boundaries of things, just like the hawthorn, which only adds to its magical reputation. In 'The Triads of Ireland' the elder is one of the three possible tokens of a cursed site (although in this text the Gaelic word for elder tree is tromm, not ruis).[64] Elder blossoms are one of the specific items mentioned in A Tract on the Plague as a scent that can increase the 'humours in the body', probably what we would refer to now as boosting our immune system.[65] According to Rosa Anglica, the inner bark could be eaten to make a man vomit to help ease abscesses on the testicles![66] Grim stuff, and surprising, as the same text tells us that elder is also useful for hernia, without any real connection between the two medical applications being made. J.K. Rowling in her Harry Potter series has the most powerful wand being made of elder wood; it's worth bearing in mind that to do this one would need to do significant damage to the tree, as the hard wood all comes from the heart wood or the thick roots.

Animals

Corvids: Crows, rooks, ravens, jackdaws, magpies and jays. Crows are the most prominent corvid in Celtic mythology and earlier in this book you will find a detailed description of my own experiences with crows. Ravens are generally revered as the 'wisest' of birds whereas crows are associated with magic and mystery. I think this fits very well; crows may not be as 'intellectual' but they have a keen instinct and a firm foot (talon) in both this world and the 'otherworld', the world beyond the veil that we can't see. They have strong family ties and usually mate for life. So it's simple to associate crows with loyalty, magic, spirits (or things that lie beyond what we can see, not necessarily the dead, just the 'not here') and points of change such as dusk and dawn.

I particularly associate crows with dusk as they tend to be more visible at this time. Crows are also associated with death; from a Celtic perspective they are associated with the Morrigan and her counterparts and she is a goddess that brings pain and death. Also, the crow is a carrion eater and therefore the end of every battle in the British Isles will have been lorded over by feasting crows seeking out the soft bits. So this association with the morbid is inevitable, but as well as death and rot, one can also see that there is a more practical association with the *living* – things die, but the living have to live, and eat, so let's not waste what's there!

The link between the living and the dead is also present in an idea some of us share: that the crow can pass between the veil at will, and is even one of the Morrigan's messengers, carrying the dead to where they need to be. When I see a crow I will always greet them and if I see two or three together I may name them for Badb, Macha and Nemain; not that I think she (or them, or the Morrigan, or any of the counterparts) is/are there, actually residing in the crows, but the crows remind me of her (their) presence, and give me a reassurance that this presence can be felt in the simplest of things. Crows are beautiful and sleek and may also be associated with vanity and cruelty, but perhaps unthinking cruelty – carelessness rather than malice. Quick thinking and mischief are also on the menu when you are dealing with the crow.

Cats: Although these days cats are synonymous with familiars and companion animals, in Celtic mythology they do not appear so frequently, and when they do it is always as fabulous and fantastic creatures, highly anthropomorphised. One example is the legend of the Cat Sídhe which is either a spectral black cat with a white mark on its chest, or a sorceress that has transformed herself into a cat. This huge beast is now said to roam the Scottish wilds. There is also a legend of the tribe of cats, lorded over by Irusan. In one tale, Seanchan the chief poet (Ard-Filé), speaks a terrible satire over Irusan because the cat in the house where he is feasting has failed to kill the mice that stole the egg he wished to eat.

> *Irusan, monster of claws, who strikes at the mouse, but lets it go; weakest of cats. The otter did well who bit off the tips of thy progenitor's ears, so that every cat since is jagged-eared. Let thy tail hang down; it is right, for the mouse jeers at thee.*[67]

Irusan hears the satire and vows revenge, and Seanchan becomes afraid. We can see from the tale that although clearly the cat is a household animal (perhaps not a pet but a working, practical animal) it is also revered as something much more than that. Unfortunately for the cat, in this 19th century version of this Irish fairy tale Irusan is killed by St Kieran and Seanchan curses the saint for it, because if Irusan had eaten him it would have reflected poorly on the king who was hosting the feast, which was Seanchan's ultimate goal!

One of the most famous surviving monuments of ancient Ireland is the Cat Stone on the Hill of Uisneach, the supposed centre of Ireland. Oweynagat – the cave of cats (also known as the Cave of Cruachan), appears in Fled Bricrend; great wildcats emerge from the mysterious cave only to be tamed by Cú Chulainn.[68] At first it's hard to understand why cats were such a mysterious creature to the Celts; the Romans were already domesticating them by this time, and there had been much contact between the Celts and the Romans. Perhaps because the cat was a relatively new addition to Celtic life, if present at all, there was still much mystery surrounding the beast's origins.

Seeing as how the crow and the bull were so revered, and these were everyday creatures, I guess it's only reasonable that an animal that was new and interesting should have even more mystery surrounding it. So if you are to stick with the original Celtic views, cats are associated with mystery, guarding the underworld, fear, transformation, superstition and nightmares. They should be treated with courtesy and respected as sentient. More modern associations are with magic, witchcraft, companionship, bravery and hunting; also to balance this laziness, viciousness and fickleness.

If you are using the cat as a representative animal in something like a card reading it's worth remembering both the 'positive' and 'negative' sides; bravery, a seemingly positive side of the cat, is not always what is required. Conversely, some situations *do* call for a little feline viciousness. Try not to get bogged down in what is 'good' and 'bad'; apply the associations to the situation correctly and the answers should be clear.

Dogs and Hounds: When one of the greatest heroes in this mythological cycle is called 'the Hound of Ulster' it should come as no surprise that the Celts and the Irish in particular are very fond of dogs and they pop up numerous times throughout their history and legends. Dogs in Celtic artwork tend to have the look of the greyhound about them (long and sleek), but there's no way to say for sure what breeds were kept, perhaps several and it was just fashionable to depict them all in a similar way. Dogs were used in battle and for hunting, and of course as companions. There are tales lingering even today in the Scottish highlands that to hit a dog is to be cursed, even paralysed.[69] Though 'loyalty' is the most common association with the dog today, perhaps looking at the animal as it was in Celtic times we could replace that with 'symbiosis'. The dog was a part of the human's life and worked for them just as the human provided for it. The dog was necessary to the human and vice versa; it was not a one-way relationship.

We can therefore think of the dog as representing the things in life that we need and should therefore nurture and nourish; not the things we like to have, but the things we can't do without. Also, we can see the symbol of the dog as perhaps representing co-dependence and that sometimes too much co-dependence can be damaging or dangerous. The dog is also strong, courageous and playful, but vicious if cornered and prone to madness and rage.

Bulls: One of the most famous pieces of evidence of how significant the bull is in Celtic culture is Táin Bó Cúailnge which translates as 'the driving off of the cows of Cooley' but is more simply known as 'The cattle raid of Cooley'. The bull, as mentioned previously in the section on Celtic creatures, is seen as the main 'object' which differentiates between Medb and Ailill: Medb (my namesake!) believes she is every bit as rich and powerful as Ailill, but he has Finnbhennach, a fertile bull who used to belong to Medb but scorned her and moved to Ailill's herd.

There are several aspects to this tale that already show the import placed on the beast. Firstly, it has a name. How many cattle herders give individual creatures names? And, if they do, it certainly shows a high degree of affection or respect placed upon the animal. Secondly, the bull is given almost human characteristics by the way it is described as 'choosing' to live among Ailill's cows. If this were a true account, perhaps Ailill moved the bull himself and chose to let Medb believe the bull had moved of his own accord, or perhaps the herds were kept close together and the bull simply was more often with the cows of Ailill. Medb decides to go after Donn Cúailnge, an equally magnificent bovine, to make herself at least equal with Ailill.[70]

As well as a rich mortal possession, it seems bulls were also special enough to be offered to the gods. Pliny relates that druids offered two cows up as sacrifices to invoke fertility, and he also comments that the bull is majestic and 'forms the most worthy and sumptuous Offering of Reconciliation to the Gods'.[71] Pliny may have been referring to a Celtic ritual he saw in Gaul or he may have made the whole thing up! But there is another aspect of the magical nature of the bull shown in the tales of the Tarbhfhess which more or less translates as 'Bull Sleep'. The druids choose a man, sacrifice a bull and make the man eat the flesh. He then sleeps while the druids watch and chant. His dreams are supposed to give the identity of the rightful King of Ireland.[72]

Cows: Whereas the bull seems to be a symbol of wealth, power and perhaps even fertility, the cow seems more a symbol of magic. The Morrigan transforms herself into a heifer at the head of a stampede during her interference in one of Cú Chulainn's fights in Táin Bó Cúailnge, and manages to wound him. In the aftermath of this, she appears as an old woman milking a cow;[73] is the cow a symbol of the magic at work here, or an attempt by the Morrigan to normalise the situation, to hide the magical aspect with mundane activity?

Tales of curses of paralysis and also of blessings of food and plenty are often found with cows either playing a background or leading role.[74] The cow seems gentle and soft eyed, but is great, powerful and a fierce mother. She feeds us and quenches our thirst, and is probably one of the most crucial animals in western culture for the past several millennia. She is a herd animal, symbolising the power of working together, and the protective warmth of family and close friends.

Eels: The most immediate reference to the eel that comes to mind is when the Morrigan becomes an eel in order to attack Cú Chulainn.[75] This seems a strange choice compared to cow and wolf; her other two choices for transformation have obvious strengths and fierceness, so why an eel? What was the significance? Cormac úa Cuinn supposedly found the three greatest drinking horns in all of Ireland and one of these was called 'The Eel', but there is no explanation as to why; perhaps it was just an eel-like shape.[76] Another wonder of Clonmacnois was a blind man who would dive into the river Shannon and return to the shore with an eel in each hand and foot.[77]

It's a newer source that maybe gives some insight into why an eel may be fearsome. According to a work done in 1911, there is a dark pool in Clondiff called 'The Eel Hole'. Local legend has it that a 'Worm' lived there; a huge beast with a head like a horse that would attack walkers on the moor![78] Now it starts to make sense. If eel was actually a common word for a great beast, just as 'worm' or 'wyrm' has been throughout the ages, then perhaps the Morrigan transformed herself into something far more terrifying than we first presume? Yes the eel is fast, slippery, sneaky and prone to hiding in the dark, but here we have an image of something not only cunning but strong and dangerous; a challenge even for the mighty Cú Chulainn.

Of course there are many, many more animals that were revered by the Celts and still are today. Hopefully some of the sources I have mentioned (definitely check out the bibliography!) will let you find more information than I have been able to impart in this small section. Go and find out about snakes in Ireland, or the salmon of wisdom, and most of all think about what these animals mean to us today.

Appendix C

A Few Key Figures and Beings from Celtic Mythology

Cú Chulainn: The hero of the Ulster Cycle, Cú Chulainn is a fierce warrior who performs superhuman deeds from a very young age. He is the epitome of what it is to find your limits and go beyond them, to create yourself in the image you wish to see. He takes responsibility for his actions; when he has killed a guard dog in self-defence, he offers to take its place and be the new protector, thus earning his nickname of 'Hound'. He is strong, and brave, but he makes grave mistakes and can be harsh and dismissive.

Out of all the characters in the Ulster Cycle, Cú Chulainn is probably the most accessible, and has been written about many times, and has many statues and images depicting his feats. He is so revered as an Irish hero that he has even appeared on their currency. He is unique in being a hero to both Irish Nationalists and Ulster Unionists.

Banshee: The familiar term 'banshee' comes from the old Irish Bean Sí (Sídhe) or 'Woman of the Mounds', literally a female member of Tuatha Dé Danann. The term has become commonly used to describe a creature from the otherworld who begins to wail when someone is about to die. The etymology makes sense because Celtic women would perform what is known as 'keening' to mourn the loss of someone, as is described when Brigid loses her son on the battlefield.[79] The otherworldly, super-natural aspect comes into play when we realise this particular 'bean sídhe' does not *wait* for the person to die before starting the keening: very disconcerting.

There are Scottish tales of a banshee washing the bloodstained clothes of those about to die. To me this is clearly a reference to the Morrigan who, as I previously discussed with Chris, must have a great deal to do with the creation of this legend. Chris mentioned that the banshee is only attached to particular families and upon research it seems that it was quite an honour to have a banshee announce the upcoming demise of a family member as apparently it indicates the family is of some noble or ancient descent.[80]

Families would often have keeners to sing death laments for their lost ones. The legend of a supernatural creature seems to have begun when these families were reputed to have a keener who would start wailing the death lament for a lost family member before anyone was notified of the death, thus creating the reputation of a fairy woman.

The banshee is an immensely popular figure in modern popular culture, appearing in X-Men as a mutant with super-human sonic abilities, a wailing aircraft in the Xbox game series Halo, and as the more familiar supernatural shrieking creature in Harry Potter. To me, she represents not only the pain of loss but the gift of precognition and the ability to warn those you love of things that are heading their way. She also symbolises resigning yourself to that which you know you cannot change; she is acceptance.

Sídhe: Sídhe (sounds like Shee) or Sí is an interesting term because really it is not a person, but a place; the place becomes so strongly associated with the beings in question though, that they take on the name forever after. Really we should say Aes Sídhe, the people of the mounds, the mounds being where the halls of the beings lay, hidden from earthly view. You are most likely to encounter the Aes Sídhe at dawn or dusk, when it is neither light nor dark and the world hangs at a point of change.

So who are they? The Tuatha Dé Danann, driven from the 'real world' by the Milesians and living what is both seen as underground and a completely different dimension altogether; somewhat like the Christian heaven or hell. Both are described as above and below us respectively, yet neither can be seen in this life; they exist beyond our mortal experience. The halls of the Sídhe are rather like this. Although the mounds themselves are real, often burial mounds, the inhabitants are nowhere to be seen, as they are living their own full and interesting lives somewhere slightly beyond what we refer to as physical.

Bres: Bres (meaning beautiful), like Lugh, was born of a Fomorian father and a Danann mother: Elatha and Eri.[81] He was supposed to be the king who patched things up between the Tuatha Dé Danann and the Fomorians after their first big bust up, and was married to Brigid as a symbol of that unity. But he was a poor leader, a bad host, and even inspired the first political satire Ireland had seen. He defects to the Fomorians, thinking better to lead them to victory than stay an unloved king, but he loses and is spared only by the mercy of Lugh.

Bres symbolises things going wrong, and that sometimes it is better to stick with what seems a bad lot and make the best of it than to constantly be trying to find something better, something grander, or an easy way out. He particularly highlights that power may be attractive, but that power brings responsibility and respect is to be earned from others, not demanded. Although it seems there is little positive about Bres' story, when Lugh spares his life Bres promises to teach the Tuatha Dé Danann about agriculture, a great gift that would have far reaching benefits. Perhaps this shows us that out of the darkest experiences there can spring hope, new beginnings and that there is always a chance for a fresh start.

Óengus: Mentioned earlier in this book in the section on dreams, Óengus is the son of the Dagda and Boann, and is associated with love, youth, healing and poetry. His skill with words is displayed when he tricks his father out of his home, by using the term 'day and night' to imply only one day and night's ownership, when in reality he meant *all* days and nights, and thus he moves into the Dagda's home forever.

He is also prone to violent rage, in one instance to protect the reputation of his brother, and in another instance against his foster mother for interfering with his woman. Óengus is a powerful but fickle being; if he is kept happy, he is a loyal protector, but he is temperamental and clever with it, so must not be underestimated. He reminds us to control our emotions, and not to let them control us. He shows us the importance of family and loyalty, but also his actions are a reminder not to be blinded by that loyalty. Act with honesty and guidance and do not react out of fear or loathing.

Morrigan: Renowned as a triple goddess of war, sex and prophecy, as mentioned early on in this book, she has many more facets than this. In story she appears in many different guises, and reminds us that we all have that power: to transform ourselves, to shape our own existence; we simply have to take that power and use it.

Strongly associated with fire due to the imagery of red hair and her confrontational attitude, I also find her an 'earthy' deity; she can be very grounding as she strips away your illusions about yourself, and makes you see things honestly, even if that's quite painful.

Her most well-known aspects are Macha, Badb and Nemain, and she appears as a young woman, an old woman, and in many animal forms as well. Her most well-known form is the crow, although sometimes this is her companion too. The red in her hair associates her with magic, and she represents binding oaths and transformation.

Lugh: Son of Cían, he is often seen as a sun god and is described as literally shining. He is skilled in many crafts and music, and can be a patron to those looking to master a particular skill. He is a great leader and warrior, and although he is born of two opposing sides his loyalties never waver and, indeed, he is firm yet generous with his enemies. Because of his mixed parentage he is sometimes seen as a symbol of balance, and the union of opposing forces or opposite natures. He can help you balance your own dual nature if you are in two minds about something.

He is also sometimes seen as having three aspects, almost like a triple god, and one of his origin stories names him as one of three triplets; the other two either die or are never heard from again. This, I think, is a way of looking at the many aspects of a very complex man and god, and if you are to bring Lugh into your life, I think it is important to look at the many aspects of yourself and be comfortable with them all; accept yourself as a whole person made up of many different characteristics and talents.

Dagda: A father figure, a great leader: strong, forgiving; accepting of mistakes as long as you can learn from them; sexual, impulsive and loving. He is the representation of what we love about where we are now, and what we can do to keep it a wonderful, warm place to be.

He is a great musician and a good patron for musicians, particularly stringed instruments, and particularly gentle, soothing music. Although he is a war leader, he fights because he has to, to protect his land and his people. Ultimately he is a man/god of peace, protection and healing, and when you drink from his cauldron your fears and pains are washed away.

Boann: Mother of Óengus, her name means 'white cow', again pointing to the magical reverence the Celts placed upon the cow. She is supposed to have created the River Boyne in Leinster, Ireland. Her husband had forbidden her to approach the Well of

Wisdom, so as we often do when forbidden to do something interesting, she went out of her way to disobey. The magic of the well was indicated by the hazel trees growing around it, and the salmon living within. Boann's pride caused her to walk around the well 'widdershins' or anti-clockwise, thus challenging the magical power held within the waters of the well. They reacted somewhat violently, erupting and dragging her down to the sea, creating the River Boyne and maiming her horrifically.

She is also known as a protector of mortals, and is capable of showing and inspiring great passion, as shown by her affair with the Dagda. He stopped the sun for nine months so no one would know he had lain with her and that she had borne his son. Boann is about desire and pride, and doing things despite our better judgement. We can see this as encouragement to follow our instincts, and also as a help to curb them when necessary.

Brigid: Patron of bards, smiths and mothers, she is all about creation. Honoured at Imbolc, she is representative of the springtime because of this connection to creativity, which of course is linked to the creation of new life and the warmth returning to the world with the new season. Appropriate offerings are oatcakes and milk and anything homemade really. She appreciates the effort you will go to in order to give her honour; making something yourself is a sacrifice of your time and this is a real sacrifice to her. She appreciates the precious gift of every second and teaches you to appreciate it too.

Scáthach: Scáthach is the woman who teaches Cú Chulainn about war, combat and most significantly about the use of the unique spear, the Gae Bulg or Gae Bolga. She is supposedly Scottish, fierce and wild, but disciplined and educated in militant arts. She becomes involved sexually with Cú Chulainn, as does her twin and her daughter; perhaps these are all different aspects of the same woman?

Scáthach seems to me to represent all that is worldly and non-magical; mundane yet precious. She is the family you will fight for, the food you make to fill your belly and the sport you play that keeps you fit and happy. She will help you find justice and wants you to take pride in your abilities. She encourages you to excel, find balance, and be strong in the face of your adversaries.

Cernunnos: Cernunnos is depicted on the Pillar of the Boatmen, a stone bas relief dated to the 1st Century CE, as a deity with stag horns bearing torques, such as the ones found at Celtic sites. This is the only time he is named Cernunnos, but a similar figure appears on the Gundestrup Cauldron which possibly dates back to 200 BC. Both figures are horned, and bear torques, and on the Cauldron he is surrounded by beasts, including a stag that has nearly identical horns.

Not much else is known about his history, but he has become synonymous with the Horned God, the lord of the land, the male side of god or nature, and the spirit of woods and the beasts within. Sometimes he is connected to Herne, and certainly he does seem to have a streak of wildness one associates with the hunt; a fierce energy and focus that can be overwhelming. There's so little evidence he was ever worshipped in the British Isles, but I know I'm certainly not the only one who has named a fierce, wild, male energy 'Cernunnos'.

Glossary of Gaelic Terms

I include these as a point of interest for anyone reading Celtic literature or interested in the old Irish myths and legends. There's no *need* to know these words and phrases really, as most works have been translated, and of course Gaelic to English dictionaries are readily available, but it's interesting to see how some of the words and phrases have leaked into modern English usage, and also the more obscure roots of some now everyday phrases.

Thomas MacDonald, in his 1926 book Gaelic Proverbs and Proverbial Sayings, observed that '…the Celtic races were not much given to proverbs, and the explanation given is that a people gifted with the power of speech, like the Celts, are averse to their too frequent use.'[82] Looking at some of the proverbs given, I can see what he means by the 'power of speech' and agree that perhaps we bandy words about too easily, forgetting the great power they can have. Have a look at some of the proverbs below, and decide for yourself if the words are powerful, clever or simply an example of how the Celts (Irish and Scottish in these examples) loved to use metaphor to transform one thing into another.

Animals
Torc: Pig
Tarbh: Bull
Bo: Cow
Badb: Crow
Cíaróg: Beetle
Nathair: Adder
Snáthaid: Dragonfly
Iolar: Eagle
Coileach: Cockerel

Lacha: Duck

Eilit: Hind

Damh: Stag or Ox, very confusing. Possibly just means horned beast. Carria or Charria can also be used for Stag, Buck or Hart, as can Poic although this can also mean a Goat.

Luch: mouse

Familiar Words

Sláinte: Used as the toast 'Cheers!' but literally means 'health' as in wishing health upon the person/persons you are toasting. Sounds like Slan-Cha.

Taing: Thanks. Taingealas means thankfulness and sounds very similar.

Geas: A binding oath often seen as a spell or sorcery. If one is 'under a geas' one is bound by the terms of that geas, for example, famously Cú Chulainn could not eat dog meat because it was his totem animal.

Bràthair: Brother

Geill: Yield

Geata: Gate

Graing: Disdain, Frown. Perhaps an early version of 'grumpy'?

Grainnsear: Farmer. Literally 'The Grain Sir'. The man who deals with the grain.

Grap: Dung fork. Interestingly close to our word 'crap' although the etymological history points to Dutch and French origins. Considering the Celts moved across Europe, the Gaelic may have the same roots as the French and Dutch anyway.

Seanfhocal: Proverbs

Scileann fíon fírinne. Wine lets out the truth.

Fillean meal ar an meallaire. Evil returns to the evil-doer.

Aithníonn ciaróg ciaróg eile. One beetle recognizes another beetle, the root of the more common 'it takes one to know one'.

Nuair atá an cat amuigh bíonn na luch ag damhsa. When the cat is away, the mice will dance (play).

Bidh an t-ubhal as fheàrr air a'mheangan as àirde. The best apple is on the highest bough.

Fear sam bith a loisgeas a mhàs, 's e fhèin a dh'fheumas suidhe air. Whoever burns his backside must himself sit upon it. (A rather more graphic and amusing version of 'you made your own bed; now lie in it')

An làmb a bheir, 's i a gheibh. The hand that gives is the hand that gets.

Cha toir a'bhòidhchead goil air a' phoit. Beauty won't boil the pot.

Bibliography

1, 3, 16. Macalister, R. A. Stewart (translator). Lebor Gabála Érenn. (The Book of the Taking of Ireland; The Book of Invasions). Irish Texts Society, 1956. Used gratefully with the kind permission of http://www.ucc.ie/celt/ where this work is published.

2. Various authors. The Phantom Queen Awakes. Morrigan Books, 2010.

4, 25, 27, 31, 53, 59, 63, 70, 73, 75. O'Reilly, Cecile. Táin Bó Cúailnge Recension 1, 1976. Used gratefully with the kind permission of http://www.ucc.ie/celt/ where this work is published.

5. Leahy, Arthur Herbert. The Courtship of Etain from Heroic Romances of Ireland. London: David Nutt, 1905.

6. Bergin, Osborn. 'How the Dagda Got His Magic Staff.' Medieval Studies in Memory of Gertrude Schoepperle Loomis. NY: Columbia University Press, 1927.

7, 11, 13, 29, 32. Gregory, Lady Augusta. Gods and Fighting Men: The story of the Tuatha de Danaan and of the Fianna of Ireland, arranged and put into English. 1905.

8, 56. Stokes, Whitley (translator). Lives of Saints, from The Book of Lismore. Clarendon Press, 1890.

9. Stokes, Whitley (translator). Cormac's Glossary, Codex A. Williams and Norgate, 1862.

10, 24, 79. Gray, Elizabeth (translator). Cath Maige Tuired: The Second Battle of Mag Tuired. 1982, Irish Texts Society. Used gratefully with the kind permission of http://www.ucc.ie/celt/ where this work is published.

12. Farady, L. Winifred M. A. (translator). The Cattle Raid of Cuailnge (Táin Bó Cúailnge). David Nutt. 1904.

14, 34. Dearg Doom from The Táin, Horslips, 1973, Horslips Records. Lyrics used with kind permission of Shay Hennessy of

Crashed Music and Jim Lockhart of Horslips. Thanks guys.

15. Dance of Brigid from Laying it Down, Mabh Savage, 2012.

17, 18. Brand, John; Ellis, Henry, Sir. Observations on the Popular Antiquities of Great Britain. Henry G. Bohn, 1853.

19. Coligny Calendar indicates that Celts divided the year into simply summer and winter.

20. Pringle, Mary P. Yule-Tide in Many Lands. Boston: Lothrop. Lee & Shepard Co. 1916.

21, 37. Tacitus, Cornelius; Murphy, Arthur. Historical Annals of Cornelius Tacitus. L. Johnson, Philadelphia, 1832.

22. Sideways to the Sun from The Book of Invasions: A Celtic Symphony, Horslips, 1976, Horslips Records. Lyrics used with kind permission of Shay Hennessy of Crashed Music and Jim Lockhart of Horslips. Thanks again!

23, 40. Stokes, Whitley (translator). Cu Chulainn's Death from Revue Celtique, Tome 3. Paris: F. Vieweg, 1878.

26. Muller, Ed. The Dream of Oengus (Aislinge Oengusso) from Revue Celtique, Tome 3. Paris: F. Vieweg, 1878.

28. McGarry, Gina. Brighid's Healing: Ireland's Celtic Medicine Traditions. Green Magic, 2000.

30, 36, 60. Leahy, Arthur Herbert. The Apparition of the Great Queen to Cuchulain from Heroic Romances of Ireland (taken from The Yellow Book of Lecan). London: David Nutt, 1905.

33. The Warm Sweet Breath of Love from The Book of Invasions: A Celtic Symphony, Horslips, 1976, Horslips Records. Lyrics used with kind permission of Shay Hennessy of Crashed Music and Jim Lockhart of Horslips. Thanks again!

35. You Can't Fool the Beast from The Táin, Horslips, 1973, Horslips Records. Lyrics used with kind permission of Shay Hennessy of Crashed Music and Jim Lockhart of Horslips. Once again, thank you so much!

38, 44, 54. O'Keeffe, James G. Buile Suibhne (The Frenzy of Suibhne). Being the Adventures of Suibhne Geilt. A Middle-Irish Romance. London: Irish Texts Society, 1904. Used gratefully with the kind permission of http://www.ucc.ie/celt/ where this work is published.

39, 77. Todd, James Henthorn. The Irish Version of the Historia Britonum of Nennius. Dublin: Irish Archaeological Society, 1848.

41. Mac Neill, Eoin. The Rowan Tree of Clonfert, Duanaire Finn: The Book of the Lays of Fionn. London: David Nutt, 1908.

42, 51, 58, 81. Gwynn, Edward. Translation of The Metrical Dindshenchas. CELT, 2010. Used gratefully with the kind permission of http://www.ucc.ie/celt/ where this work is published.

43, 48, 50, 52. Keating, Geoffrey D.D. The First Book of the History of Ireland with translation and notes by David Comyn. London: St. Joseph's Hospital Library, 1902.

45. Meyer, Kuno. The Death-Tales of the Ulster Heroes. Dublin: Hodges, Figgis and Co. 1906.

46. Meyer, Kuno. Aislinge Meic Conglinne, The Vision of MacConglinne, a Middle-Irish wonder tale. London, 1892. Used gratefully with the kind permission of http://www.ucc.ie/celt/ where this work is published.

47. MacDougall, Rev. James. Folk Tales and Fairy Lore in Gaelic and English. Edinburgh: John Grant, 1910.

49. Stokes, Whitley (translator). Book of Ballymote. Used gratefully with the kind permission of http://www.ucc.ie/celt/ where this work is published.

55. Bergin, Osbourne; Best, R. I. Tochmarc Étaíne in Ériu. Dublin: Hodges Figgis. 1938. Used gratefully with the kind permission of http://www.ucc.ie/celt/ where this work is published.

57, 61. Knott, Eleanor. The Bardic poems of Tadhg Dall Ó Huiginn (1550–1591). London: Irish Texts Society, 1922.

62. Kohl, J.G. Travels in Ireland. London: Brue and Wyld, 1844.

64. Meyer, Kuno. The Triads of Ireland. Dublin: Hodges, Figgis and Co. 1906.

65. Wulff, Winifred. A Tract on the Plague. Dublin: Royal Irish Academy, 1928. Used gratefully with the kind permission of

http://www.ucc.ie/celt/ where this work is published.

66. Anglici, Johannis; Wulff, Winifred M.A. Rosa Anglica Sev Rosa Medicinae. London: Simpkin, Marshall Ltd. 1929.

67. 'Speranza', Lady Wilde. Ancient Legends, Mystic Charms and Superstitions of Ireland. Boston: Tickner and Co. 1887.

68. Henderson, George. Fled Bricrend: The Feast of Bricriu. London: Irish Text Society, David Nutt, 1899.

69, 74. Maclean, Hector. Gaelic Mythology. London: S.N. 1879

71. Holland, Dr. Philemon. Pliny's Natural History in Thirty Seven Books, Volume 1. George Barclay, 1848.

72. Draak, Maartje. Some Aspects of Kingship in Pagan Ireland from The Sacral Kingship. Netherlands: E. J. Brill, 1959.

76. Gwynn, E. J. The Three Drinking Horns of Cormac úa Cuinn [From the Liber Flavus Fergusiorum] in Ériu. Volume 2. Dublin: Royal Irish Academy, 1905. Used gratefully with the kind permission of http://www.ucc.ie/celt/ where this work is published.

78. Atkinson, E.D. Dromore, An Ulster Diocese. Royal Society of Antiquaries of Ireland, 1911. Used gratefully with the kind permission of http://www.ucc.ie/celt/ where this work is published.

80. Croker, Thomas Crofton. Fairy Legends and Traditions of the South of Ireland. London, J.Murray, 1825.

82. MacDonald, Thomas Donald. Gaelic proverbs and proverbial sayings, with English translations. Eneas Mackay Stirling, 1926.

MOON

BOOKS

Moon Books invites you to begin or deepen your encounter with Paganism, in all its rich, creative, flourishing forms.